# Three Myths of
# Gods, Devils, and Beasts

by the Rhipidon Society

"Fish cannot carry guns."

Dear Keith,
 Thanks for all your encouragement & support throughout the years and the many kindnesses you have shown me. I am deeply grateful to have such a wonderful & talented uncle!

The Pentaradial Press
P.O. Box 8318
Dallas TX 75205

Your loving nephew,
Freck

*Three Myths of Gods, Devils, and Beasts*

Copyright © 1997 by The Pentaradial Press

"Cycle of the Phoenix" © 1997 by Breck M. Outland
"The Baphomet in History and Symbolism" © 1997 by Forrest Jackson
"The Mad God's Sacraments" © 1997 by Steve Aydt

Front and back cover illustrations by Steve Aydt
Cover layout and design by Phillip Walker
Interior layout and design by Rodney Perkins

All rights reserved.

First printing: August 1997

Hardcover edition ISBN 0-9659512-2-7
Paperback edition ISBN 0-9659512-3-5

Published by
The Pentaradial Press
P.O. Box 8318
Dallas, TX 75205

http://www.pentaradial.com

# Table of Contents

| | |
|---|---:|
| Introduction | 1 |
| *Cycle of the Phoenix*<br>    Breck M. Outland | 5 |
| *The Baphomet in History and Symbolism*<br>    Forrest Jackson | 45 |
| *The Mad God's Sacraments*<br>    Steve Aydt | 75 |
| Bibliography | 137 |

# Introduction

Consisting primarily of the legends of the gods, mythology is a spiritual and moral map by which to chart a course through life. Quaint as some myths may be, mythology is not limited to the recounting of fairy tales. Instead, it is an informational structure that both teaches and guides those who believe the substance of the fables. To fully understand a myth, one must empirically experience its truth first-hand. The founders of the ancient Mystery Religions understood the necessity of such direct revelatory experiences, so they incorporated instructive mythologies into their ceremonies in order to open the initiates' eyes to the beauties of Nature and of God. Today, few people actually believe the myths of the ancients. Instead, some choose to believe the myths of the present era, such as the enigmas surrounding the UFO phenomenon. So, even though mythologies may adapt themselves to fit new circumstances, they remain part of humanity's search for meaning. In this way, modern metaphors continue to validate the spiritual essence of mythology eternally.

Somewhat akin to the ancient celebrants of the Mysteries, the Rhipidon Society is a collective devoted to achieving the unmediated experience of God. It consists of more people than the authors of this book. Indeed, any soul who seeks divine knowledge may be considered a member of the Society. The appellation comes from Phillip K. Dick's transcendent science fiction novel, *VALIS*. Before traveling to Northern California to meet God, incarnated as Sophia (the Goddess of wisdom), the characters group themselves as the Rhipidon Society. They arrived at the name after reflecting upon an autobiographical character's vision:

## Three Myths

> Fat told us of a dream he had had recently, in which he had been a large fish. Instead of an arm he had walked around with sail-like or fan-like fins; with one of these fins he had tried to hold onto an M-16 rifle but the weapon had slipped to the ground, whereupon a voice had intoned: "Fish cannot carry guns." Since the Greek word for that kind of fan was *rhipidos* — as with Rhiptoglossa reptiles – we finally settled on the Rhipidon Society, the name referring elliptically to the Christian fish. This pleased Fat, too, since it alluded back to the Dogon people and their fish symbol for the benign deity.

Significantly, in early 1974 a chance glimpse of the Christian fish symbol touched off a lingering Gnostic experience that sent Dick on a quest to understand every facet of God. He wrote of his divine theories in a 10,000 (or more) page manuscript known as the *Exegesis*. Throughout the journal and the novel based on it, his writing bounces between limpidity and insanity. Apparently, achieving gnosis is not without its perils, as he wrote in the novel:

> An interruption from the collective unconscious, Jung taught, can wipe out the fragile individual ego. In the depths of the collective archetype slumber; if aroused, they can heal or they can destroy. This is the danger of archetypes; the opposite qualities are not yet separated. Bipolarization into paired opposites does not occur until consciousness occurs. So, with the gods, life and death — protection and destruction — are one. This secret partnership exists outside of time and space. It can make you very much afraid, and for good reason. After all, your existence is at stake.

But, the fact that Phillip K. Dick, to some degree, lost his mind does not negate the importance of his discoveries and revelations. After all, in the ancient times mentioned above, insanity was sometimes viewed as a gift from God, rather than as a curse. And though he suffered terribly, Dick's madness can ac-

## *Three Myths*

tually be interpreted as a similarly great and divine gift. He was more than a good novelist. He was a great myth maker.

So, one of the goals of the present Rhipidon Society is to overtax the rational mind until one sees God. But, while glimpsing into the abyss of madness, it is important to maintain some standards of objectivity. The faiths that supply the Society's pantheon of archetypes are varied. Sufism, mystic Christianity, Freemasonry, Qabalism, Hinduism, Hedonism, and Humanism all converge to render the broadest possible understanding of religion. A more specific goal of the Society is to induce mystical states of consciousness, by whatever means necessary, and to share these insights with those who are willing to receive knowledge of them.

Accordingly, the present volume is designed as a rollercoaster of esoteric ideology. The angelic ascents and vertiginous plunges render sensible concepts that would otherwise remain obscured. With a gleeful gamboling through the annals of history, we ride through the portals of time into a funhouse of child-like speculation. There, we witness the primitive births, early adolescences, and hale adulthoods of the legends of the Phoenix, the Baphomet, and Dionysus. These fabulous beasts, devils, and gods overreach all cultures and civilizations with a triple leap of allegory. And, by explicating their individual meanings, we can better appreciate our place in the universe from a vista of greater understanding.

# Cycle of the Phoenix
# by Breck M. Outland

With its ever present protection and warmth, fire has been our companion through the predatorial nights from the earliest recollection we have as humans. An intangible fear also exists of fire's terrible, destructive power, which is tempered only by our abilities to harness its energy for creation. As from time immemorial, at every dawn the joyous return of the sun dictates our daily and seasonal rhythms, bestowing its dazzling gift on what would otherwise be a dark, lifeless planet. Its appearance provides a governing order and model of regularity in an otherwise chaotic existence. It is certainly no wonder that numerous sacred myths and legends attempt to interpret and explain the fundamental forces of the sun and fire. They have encompassed so many facets of our being, just as they have given us our first cognizance of a harmonious universal balance. Without the

## Three Myths

benevolent radiance of the sun, all life would fall into cold eternal night. Thus, every natural form of life, in its own way, must humbly obey the solar cadence. This empirical observation prompted early civilizations to affiliate the sun as the flaming throne from which divine vital energies descend to all living creatures, and from which fire itself comes. Even now, by staring into the dancing flames of an evening campfire, we can easily transport ourselves into the trance-like awe that early tribal races must have felt in connection with the ominous power of fire. The concepts of fire, the sun, and eternal renewal have continued in the personification of a most imaginative and inspiring mythical beast, traditionally known as the Phoenix.

The emblem of the Phoenix is familiar to most people, in this present age, as a common trademark emblazoned on TransAm and Firebird sports cars. With its bold graphic figure of sleek wings and a noble head rising from the stylized flames, it seems to represent, at least for the automobile industry, a marketing tactic to capture the imagination and vigor of youth in order to resurrect a diminishing cash flow. In the United States today there are hundreds of corporations, dealing in everything from high technology to standard insurance, that make daily use of the image of the Phoenix as their logotype without the slightest understanding of its origins. In short, the Phoenix has been relegated to the position of just another promotional device. But, as a long-held solar icon of renewal and rebirth, the Phoenix's inspiration permeates many cultures and time periods, including the present. It is as everlasting as the ideology its endlessly repeated image suggests. Though much of this regal bird's true legendary significance remains submerged or obscured, it still burns in our subconscious, as its symbol achieves wider and wider circulation in our phenomenal world. By examining the cycle of the Phoenix, it is possible to unearth some fragments of meaning that still remain from its diverse conceptual sources.

According to most of the various stories, the Phoenix is a bird approximately the size of a large eagle. It has brilliantly colored plumage of either plum tint with a golden collar and a scarlet tail or an overall dazzling mixture of red, gold, and blue. One

## Three Myths

explanation for the difference in descriptions is that its feathers may be imagined as changing coloration throughout its long life; marking the stages of its progress. This rare bird is the only one of its kind and supposedly lives in Arabia. At the end of an epoch, such as the one approaching, it feels its death drawing near and fashions a nest or pyre of the most fragrant boughs and cinnamon bark, on which it then sits and sings a song of hauntingly magnificent beauty. Then the heated rays of the sun ignite the nest, and both this pyre and the bird are consumed in flames until only cinders remain. From the ashes arises a worm, representing the archetypal soul, which subsequently and quickly grows into another renewed Phoenix.

Gifted with a vague sort of fiery parthenogenesis, it is simultaneously both its own parent and child. A Grecian statue of Hermaphroditus, now located in the British Museum, shows the androgynous god feeding grapes to a bird that strongly resembles the Phoenix; emphasizing the bisexual principle of its regeneration. The first series of tasks that the newly revitalized bird must accomplish is to gather the ashes of its previous incarnation (or ancestral spirit), to enclose them in an egg-like ball of myrrh, and to fly away with it. Accompanied by a procession of other birds to Anu (or Heliopolis, the City of the Sun) on the Nile in Egypt, the Phoenix is received by the priests of the temple and with great ceremony the mummified egg is interred upon the altar of Ra, the sun god. In Egyptian lore the egg symbolizes the soul of the world or Cosmic Egg from which the universe was created. After performing this funereal ritual, the Phoenix then returns to its home to live out its own course of life. Regarding the length of its life, some accounts cite 1461 years as its life cycle, while most others favor an interval of no less than 500 years.

One prominent version of the Phoenix myth stems from ancient Greek literature. In Herodotus' account of his journeys in Egypt (circa 430 BC), he reports from Heliopolis, where he saw paintings of the bird. Its very name may be due to a confusion with the date palm (*phoenix dactylifera*), a tree upon which the bird is often depicted. This tree is also known as *phoinix* in Greek. The Phoenicians derive the name of their country from this source and from the celebrated purple dyes made from the local murex mollusk, which were highly prized in the ancient world. Another derivation of the Greek word *phoinix* is "purple-red." In somewhat later versions of the legend, the immortal bird returns to Phoenicia to live out its life, rather than dissappearing to the deserts of Arabia. This shift of location could be attributed to the immigration into Syria and Palestine by large groups of ancient races from Arabia and the Persian Gulf during the third and second millenia BC, most probably bringing their local legends along with them. It is only later, in the fourth century AD, that the fiery aspects of its death were added in two poems about the Phoenix by Claudian and Lacantius. Translator Henry Vaughn describes the scenario:

> He knows his time is out! and does provide
> New principles of life; herbs he brings dried
> From the hot hills, and which rich spices frames
> A Pile shall burn, and hatch him with his flames.
>
> On this the weakling sits; salutes the Sun
> With pleasant noise, and prays and begs for some
> Of his own fire, that quickly may restore
> The youth and vigor, which he had before.
>
> Whom soon as Phoebus spies, stopping his reigns
> He makes a stand, and thus allays his pains...
> He shakes his locks, and from his golden head,
> Shoots one bright beam, which smites with vital fire
> The willing bird; to burn is his desire,
> That he may live again; he's proud in death,
> And goes in haste to gain a better breath.
>
> The spicy heap fired with celestial rays
> Does burn the aged Phoenix, when straight stays
> The Chariot of the amazed Moon; the pole
> Resists the wheeling, swift Orbs, and the whole
> Fabric of Nature at a stand remains,
> Till the old bird a new, young being gains. [1]

*Three Myths*

Interestingly, this poem engages all of our senses completely, producing a vividly inspiring visualization of this climactic moment in the regeneration of the Phoenix. The reader experiences the beautiful sound of its song, the brilliance of color from its plumage, the scent of the kindled spices of the nest, and most notably the flash of blazing heat from its self-immolation. With this excellent depiction of the death of the Phoenix fixed in our minds, the legend becomes perceptually realized. The Phoenix is a being with complete control over its own destiny. But what of the earlier legends that inspired the Greek scholars to embellish upon such a tale? Herodotus' accounts of the sacred bird at Anu (Heliopolis) points us in the right direction. For in the Egyptian Book of the Dead, which is concerned with the individual soul's safety in the journey of the afterlife, the bennu bird appears repeatedly with many of the same aspects as the Phoenix. In Egyptian mythology, the bennu is also referred to as the *bird of return*. It was associated as a familiar of Thoth in the form of the ibis, which is how the bennu is represented in hieroglyph by all their sacred texts. Thoth, the god of learning and knowledge, is most often depicted with the head of an ibis. In Greek mythology his equivalent is Hermes, the messenger of the gods. Since the ibis is a wading bird, it is possible that the bennu/phoenix inherited some of its fiery legend from a glowing phenomenon known in marshy areas as a will o' the wisp. These strange lights are, in most cases, caused by ignition of natural gases that emanate from decaying plant matter. The reedy banks of the Nile where the ibis wades could certainly be a prime spot for this natural occurrence. Moreover, the ibis, perhaps frightened by the sudden luminous flash, or maybe even set alight itself, might be seen taking a hasty flight over the water from the direction of the ball of flame.

The Egyptian Bennu

The name of the ibis in Egyptian is Tekh, the hard form of Tesh, meaning a boundary or limit. This marker refers to a border in the renewal of the lunar phases. Tekh is another name of Thoth, and Tekhi --the feminine form-- is the name of the Egyptian goddess who presided over the feminine lunar cycles or menses. This links the bennu with both the male and female forms of Thoth. Tekhi was also known as Ta-Urt, the Mother of Revolutions. In this form her name is still known in the word Tarot, or the Book of Thoth, which concerns the mysteries of Time and Cycles of Time. The Tarot has been used by seers throughout the ages as a tool for divining the future as well as reading the past. [2] With these chronological associations in mind, it will become apparent why the ibis was chosen as the glyph for the bennu, or bird of return.

In the papyrus manuscripts of Egypt, the bennu is one of the polytheistic movers of the world. As an archetypal model of the individual soul, it arises from the Isle of Fire in the underworld, which is ruled by Set (or Sothis) and flies to Anu to announce the new millennium, in which the sun renews itself. From an Egyptian astronomical perspective, the "renewal of the sun" we now know refers to the Sothic cycle. Sothis (known today as Sirius or the Dog Star) is the brightest star in the night sky. The name Sirius also comes from the Greek word meaning "scorching." At the time when Sirius made its appearance over the eastern horizon just before sunrise, it was recognized by the ancient Egyptians as the beginning of their New Year. Its rising was also an indicator of the annual flooding of the Nile River each summer. This was acknowledged as a rejuvenating of the soil around the banks for cultivation. But there was a slight discrepancy between the Egyptian calendar year of 365 days and the rising of Sothis at the beginning of the New Year. The rising of Sothis occurred at intervals of 365.25 days, so that the new year had to be advanced by an increment equal to one day for every four years. In order for the sun to return to its original conjunction or be "renewed" with Sothis, it would take a total cycle of approximately 1460 years. It is likely that this Sothic cycle was, in essence, concealed within the allegory of the Phoenix by the priests of Heliopolis in an attempt to keep this secret circular cycle hidden from their rival astronomer/priests at Thebes and Memphis. It is also worth noting that the solar year (or great year) is four years, that is, exactly 1461 days in length including Leap Year day. This computation is probably how the astronomers of the era originally understood the life cycle of the Phoenix. It also exposes the confusion introduced between years and days in the mythical bird's legendary life-span and these two solar cycles. The sun is depicted in some Egyptian carvings as a bennu flying across the heavens — reaching toward Sothis — and in this way, it is linked with Khepera, the beetle. Khepera is a symbol of the rising sun emerging from the dark underworld that is often shown holding the orb of the sun in its forelegs. The chapter in the Book of the Dead devoted to the Transformation of the Bennu is translated as follows:

> I flew up out of primeval matter. I came into being like the god Khepera. I germinated like the plants. I am concealed like the tortoise in his shell. I am the seed of every god. I am Yesterday of the Four Quarters of the Earth, and the Seven Uraei serpents, who came into being in the Eastern land. I am the Great One [Ra, Horus] who illumineth the Hememet spirits [those in the underworld] with the light of his body. I am that god in respect of Set. I am Thoth who stood between them [i.e., Horus and Set, the Sun and Sirius] as the judge on behalf of the Governor of Sekhem and the Souls of Anu [Heliopolis]. He was like a stream between them. I have come. I rise up on my throne. I am endowed with a Khu [spirit-soul]. I am mighty. I am endowed with godhood among the gods. I am Khensu, the lord of every kind of strength. [3]

Intended as a magical spell, the above incantation of the bennu was often inscribed on the outside of the sarcophagus. The spirit of the deceased one might use this spell as a method of spiritually identifying and fusing with the immortal aspects of the bennu when the soul makes its way through the treacherous underworld. In the Egyptian pantheon, the bennu is a symbol of both Ra, the sun god, and Osiris, his father, the god of resurrection. Osiris became Lord of the Underworld after his murder and dismemberment was avenged by Ra upon the dark and evil Set. Again we see the allegory for the solar cycle slowly overtaking Sirius before it sets in the West. After the murder of

## Three Myths

Osiris, his consort, Isis, gathered his various limbs except for the penis, which was lost in the waters of the Nile. After being reassembled and revived by Isis, Osiris takes on an asexual or hermaphroditic character because of this change. In the paintings of Egyptian funerary urns, a form of the bennu as heart soul (Ba) is seen hovering over the mummy of Osiris with an emblem of the sun clutched in its claws, symbolizing eternity. In this embodiment the bennu was allowed to pass freely through and out of the underworld, acting as a guiding lantern for the souls of the dead. In another section of the papyrus of Ani, the bennu is characterized as the keeper of the Tablet of Destiny, "the book of the things which have been made, and of the things which shall be made." [4] To witness and maintain the fate of mortal humankind is the natural role for a spirit-being such as the bennu to hold, being both eternal and self-perpetuating.

The Phoenix is a slain god who sacrifices itself in order to renew the vital forces of creation. It precedes mortal souls through the land of death as a guiding protector, thus ensuring the completion of the cycle of human life. And then it assumes the role of the newborn sun as it arises from the dark horizon each day. Taking flight across the whirling dome of the heavens, it keeps the planet's life in regular balance and governs its progress with divine providence. In this latter semblance as Hoo, the bird of prosperity, the Japanese associate the Phoenix with the Buddhist deity Amida, Lord of Boundless Light. Represented by a carved image in the Phoenix Hall, part of the Byodoin Temple in the suburbs of Kyoto, Amida is the ruler of the Pure Land of the afterlife who renounced becoming a Buddha until all who had offered prayers to him had attained enlightenment. Likewise, in this guise of compassionate benefactor, the Chinese identify the Phoenix as the Feng-huang whose appearance was the presage of good fortune or great events such as the turning of the millennium. The Feng-huang is like the Phoenix, in that

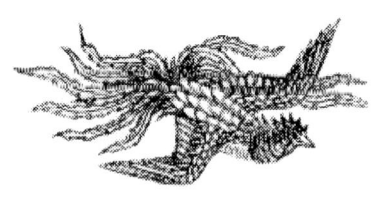

Japanese Hoo (Prosperity)

## Three Myths

both god-beasts are renowned for their songs and colorfully radiant plumage. The Feng-huang and the dragon are the most highly favored beasts in all of Chinese mythology. The Feng-huang is born from the sun or from fire and as such represents the emergence of the active principle of yang, which brings longevity to its material manifestations. The translation of *feng* means male and *huang* means female. This combination illustrates a hermaphroditic union of the aspects of yang (active) and yin (passive). This intermingling of the two aspects is not considered as duality in Oriental thought, but instead it is the blissful conjoining of heaven and earth in a perpetual consummation that brings about eternal self-regeneration.

The Chinese Feng-Huang

The etymology of the word *hermaphrodite* can give a deeper meaning to this unique form of solitary revitalization. Hermaphroditus was the son of Hermes (Mercury), Greek god of knowledge and magic, and Aphrodite (Venus), goddess of love. The combination of Aphrodite and Hermes is, in a manner of speaking, *carnal knowledge.* In brief, the myth says that when a nymph fell in love with Hermaphroditus, she became so enamored of him that she prayed to the gods that she might forever be joined with him. The resultant creation was half man, half woman. This is exactly how 15th century Christian illustrations of Adam and Eve in Eden depicted them; each having both sets of genitalia. This hermaphroditic rendering was an unusual characteristic of the perfect life in Paradise. Though it was later dropped from the Old Testament in favor of the widely known sexual duality of male and female, the concept of innocent copulation between Adam and Eve in the Garden of Eden lingers in their doctrine.

The Phoenix reappears in the prototypical Garden as the model of original innocence in the form of the Milham (or Milchaum), a Judaic legend. The Milham was one of the original mythical beasts in the Garden of Eden. As the tale goes, when Adam and

Eve ate of the Tree of Knowledge, they shared the fruit with all of the animals there. Only the Milham refused to eat and was thus rewarded by God with immortality. The Milham was protected from the Angel of Death within the walls of a specially constructed city called Luz. The entrance to Luz was unknown to all the other animals. This secret portal was supposedly hidden in an almond tree that led through a cavern to the interior of the eternal city. The Milham was described as having the purple scaly head of a crocodile, the feet and tail of a lion, and twelve shining wings. After one thousand years, the Milham's feathers would drop off and its body would shrink to the size and shape of an egg. From this egg a new Milham would hatch. Like  the Phoenix, the Milham was associated with the sun. The name of the city Luz suggests the Latin word *lux*, or light. Its duty was to fly over earth each day to protect the ground below from the scorching flames of the sun. Each night it returned to Luz. The secret passage in the almond tree also hints at a hermaphroditic metaphor, in that the shape of the almond may resemble the *vesica picis* or vagina. The tree itself is the oldest of phallic symbols. Combined together in this suggestive manner, these two sexual aspects lead to the city of Luz, or enlightenment.

Likewise, in another form of the Garden of Eden, the Phoenix plays a key role in Igor Stravinsky's *Firebird Suite*. Loosely based on a classic Russian fairy tale, the ballet spins the following yarn. The Firebird is imprisoned in the Magic Garden of the evil ogre, Kastchei the Deathless, who is virtually immortal. Kastchei has also captured thirteen Princesses from the surrounding kingdoms and is holding them hostage. Prince Ivan sneaks to the edge of the Magic Garden one enchanted night and witnesses the Firebird dancing and fluttering about on the Golden Apple Tree. Ivan catches the Firebird, but after pleas from the bird, it succeeds in being released for the price of one magic feather. The captive Princesses then appear while Ivan returns to his hiding place in the surrounding hedges to spy on them. The

## *Three Myths*

Princesses dance and play with the Golden Apples that have been christened by the Firebird. Ivan, unseen, falls in love with one of the Princesses and when their dance is over, reveals his presence. They all dance throughout the night, until dawn arrives. The Prince discovers the secret of Kastchei's mortality through the power of the Firebird, which he summons with the magic feather. Angered by the intervention of Prince Ivan, the Kastchei proclaims a battle. As Kastchei and his minions struggle with Ivan through the section called the Infernal Dance, they are finally subdued by Ivan's mastery of the power of the Firebird. The forces of evil disappear in a blazing cloud of flames and sulfur, Kastchei's kingdom is dissolved, and love triumphs. Ivan and his beloved Princess are reunited and the Firebird is left sleeping in the Magic Garden. From this fairy tale, parallels with the story of the Garden of Eden are obvious. It is only necessary to point out that the Golden Apples are the symbolic fruit of Aphrodite, the goddess of love.

The aspiration of a return to early innocence was the sole sacrament of the Brethren of the Free Spirit and the Sect of the Phoenix, heretical groups that appeared during the Middle Ages. It is thought by many historians that the Free Spirits originated as the disciples of Meister Eckhart, a Dominican monk of the 13th century, and Marguerite Porete, a Parisian beguine. Through such books as *The Mirror of Simple Souls*, the beginnings of heretical thought were passed down from the religious mystics to aristocratic Hussites or Germans of the early 14th century. Under the cloak of piousness, the goal of these secret societies was to restore within the minds of men and women the original state of innocence; that which had been lost in the Garden of Eden through nudity and pursuit of sexual pleasure. The inner nature of each initiate was granted its ultimate fulfillment by denying nothing to their desires. In this way the members achieved a state of liberated grace equaled only by the angels. The ensuing frenzy led to the rediscovery of a mystical union with universal principles that are so briefly glimpsed through the timeless window of ecstasy. To them, "the act of consecration of the host and a simultaneous sex act upon an altar were equal in spiritual worth." [5] The act of sexual intercourse was considered no more sinful than rubbing one's hands together.

## Three Myths

Much like the Tantric mystics, the intensity of orgasm was regarded as the gateway to supreme inner truth. And like the seven chakras of tantra, the practitioners of the Free Spirit pursued the "seven levels of grace," which led to the progressive union of the soul with God until the mind's very essence was dissolved in ecstasy.

The snake is often used in Tantra as a representation of rising sexual energy as it travels up from the base of the spinal column to the brain. This is what the Tantric adepts refer to as the *Layayoga* force or fire serpent. This fire serpent, or *kundalini*, slowly winds its way up from the genitals into the central nervous system. With enough mental discipline, eventually this powerful force explodes out of the crown of the head in the form of a thousand-petalled lotus, which is appropriately the color of flame. Then, in a sublime cascade of neurochemistry, the nucleated concentration of the practitioner is subjected to the blinding force of a psychic *tabula rasa*. Within this ego-negating state, the individual witnesses the most fundamental truths of their being laid bare. All living existence becomes unified in a supra-personal experience of cosmic proportion. The energized awareness of the initiate fuses with God. Unencumbered by the mundane physical world, the person is filled with holy spirit. Like the Phoenix, he or she is engulfed in the bright sun of bliss and returns from the desert of the soul to a renewed, greener life. For the Free Spirits, this fleeting source of wisdom was primarily achieved by elaborately orchestrated sexual rites that, in some ways, resemble the super-sensualist practices of the cults of Dionysus in ancient Greece. Incredibly enough, it was also believed by some Brethren members that such lasciviousness was a method for warding off the Black Plague. Many beliefs of the Sect of the Phoenix are thought to be later incarnated as the libertine Free Spirit doctrines that

## Three Myths

were carried throughout France and England by traveling gypsies. The hedonistic rituals they practiced were said to enable initiates to awaken the God within, which resulted in the exaltation of the individual, freed spirit through the profound exhaustion of the body and a suspended orgasm of the mind, or "eroto-comatose lucidity," [6] God manifested to them in all things. In the Free Spirits as well as the Sect of the Phoenix, women were worshipped as deities and were considered the vessels for divine inspiration.

Even in primitive cultures, women were said to possess fire in their genitals, which could be kindled during the friction of sexual coupling. For is not the crisis of orgasm, at its most blissful culmination, also the immolation of the ego? Are we not rejuvenated, in a sense, by the expansive insight grasped from each new erotic pleasure? According to both the Sect of the Phoenix and the Free Spirits, the soul that was annihilated in the love of the Creator, could and should "grant to nature all that it desires without remorse of conscience." [7] Perhaps this was the reason for the sect choosing the Phoenix as their icon. It is a perfect representation of purification in ecstasy and rebirth of the inner spiritual being. The Brethren of the Free Spirit believed that every stirring of delight was a revelation from God, the Creator. Like the enlightened mystics of their time, they no doubt exclaimed "rejoice, for all is ours!" The Free Spirits were not a chiliastic group, but rather the members preferred to live in the "here and now." This immediatism is perhaps a form of materialist contempt for the future torments of hell that were brandished by the orthodox clergy to subjugate the minds of the masses. These Free Spirits were also known as Adamites, since their goal was to return to the state of grace that Adam first held in Paradise. The union of the male and female in coitus was considered the most direct method for these two incomplete halves to restore the original oneness of their beings. In other words, they sought a perfection of the spirit through the balancing and reconciliation of all opposites. Within the inspired psyche of each initiate, God revealed himself in a higher mystical unity of all. This heretical concept was, in essence, their formula for transubstantiation of the host —the universal androgyne.

## Three Myths

Throughout the world, many faiths refer to a hermaphroditic or asexual source of creation. The Greeks called it the One, the Hindus named it Atman, the Qabalists call it the Smooth Point, the Gnostics, the Pleroma, and the Alchemists represented it as the Rebis. Within the 14th century Knights Templar and some contemporary mystic circles, it is known in the form of Baphomet. Whatever its name, most agree on its attributes, and that consciousness, existence, and bliss are but shadows of it that we apprehend when our illuminated minds draw near it. However this experience is attained, either through the ascetic ecstasies of the mystics — which are rare — or by the everyday mysteries of sex, the ultimate frontier of sexual pleasure is still one of the greatest areas of deliberation that persists even in our present society. Sexuality is perpetually surrounded by taboo, media titillation, and the clinical inquisition of psychoanalysis. A similar type of Inquisition that started in 1233 sought to bring an end to the explorations of these cults (such as the Sect of the Phoenix) by pronouncing their activities as "heretical." But like the bird from which they derived their name, the sect arose ever anew from the ashes of the stake; unable to be restrained within a puritanical framework. Vestiges of this obscure group supposedly survived until the 1700's.

During the early Middle Ages many bestiaries circulated throughout Europe, the Phoenix was considered by most to be a real, living bird. The Christian Church eagerly utilized the Phoenix as a symbol of the doctrine of Christ's death and resurrection. They viewed the Phoenix as a miraculous example of the proof of God's divine love for even the smallest of his creatures. Located in the Notre Dame cathedral in Paris, there is a rose window that depicts a Phoenix as the hope of Christian resurrection. The introduction of the Phoenix into Christian thought was at the behest of St. Clement, who became Bishop of Rome around 79 AD. After becoming the third pope, Clement was subsequently banished to Russia by the emperor Trajan. Trajan then commanded that the Phoenix be coined on Roman money as a symbol of the undying Roman Empire. It is significant that portions of Rome had recently been devastated in a massive fire under the rule of emperor Nero. As for St. Clement, he was later canonized as the patron saint of blacksmiths (who create from fire) after being tied to an anchor and thrown into the Black Sea. Probably, Clement's martyrdom was partly due to his introduction of what was, at that time, perceived as a heathen symbol into early Christianity.

The classical Hindu equivalent of the Phoenix is found in the likeness of Garuda, the winged beast upon which Wisnu (Vishnu) rides. In Hindu mythology, Wisnu is the god who represents the complementary aspects of continuity and order. *Garuda* is a Sanskrit word meaning "Eagle of God." Originally a solar divinity, Garuda plays a key role in some of the earliest *Puranas*, or stories of the origins. Garuda is depicted in Indonesian art as a man with bright fiery plumage, sharp talons, and the beaked head of a bird. From his fierce, eagle-like visage large fangs emerge from his beak and his eyes bulge with an animal intensity. Mythologically, this bird/man deity is the younger brother of Arjuna, the charioteer of the sun. Arjuna is equated with Apollo or Phoebus in Greek and Roman mythologies, respectively. In particular, the myth of Garuda originates in the *Adiparwa*, which dates from the tenth century AD. In this creation myth, the gods and giant demons contend for the holy water of life, or *amerta*. This water of immortality is located beneath a sea of milk, which the gods and demons churn up at Wisnu's request. This suggests an element of chaos from which order and life arise. Like Wisnu's realm of emerging order, modern chaos theory is beginning to comprehend these same principles of continuity issuing from turbulence. When the *amerta* finally does spring up out of the frothing waters, it falls on the side of the demons. But Wisnu disguises himself as a beautiful girl and talks the demons into letting her be the water-bearer. No sooner does she have the *amerta*, than she transforms back into Wisnu and runs away.

Shortly thereafter, when Garuda hatches from his egg in the aftermath from this cosmic tug-of-war between the forces of good and evil, he comes to life shining like fire, his glaring light filling the heavens in all directions. The gods panic, thinking that doomsday has arrived and that the fire will consume them. However, Agni, the god of fire, assures them that the time of the apocalypse has not yet come. It is only the powerful light of

*Three Myths*

Garuda that they behold, which is equal in brilliance only to Agni's own fiery nimbus. Garuda then takes flight, at his imprisoned mother's instructions, toward the peak of Somaka mountain where the *amerta* is kept by the gods. Only by procuring the *amerta* can Garuda hope to release his mother from her bonds. Along the way, Garuda kills and eats villains and murderers, as well as more conventional fare, such as elephants and turtles. As he methodically approaches Somaka, some of the gods try to deter Garuda from obtaining the *amerta* by attacking him, but Garuda pecks out their eyes. With blood flowing from their ocular sockets, they retreat and Garuda makes his way victoriously to the entrance of a cave where the *amerta* is hidden. Taking some water from the ocean, he then puts out the fire that burns at the entrance and rushes in to fight the two dragon guardians. After a mighty battle, Garuda finally kills and eats the dragons and takes possession of the *amerta*. As he flies away, Wisnu calls out to him and demands a favor. Wisnu asks Garuda to become his steed and messenger between heaven and earth. In this way Garuda is obliged to comply, because all favors asked, must be granted according to the laws of the gods. Garuda promises his services only after setting his mother free from her slavery. Since Wisnu also symbolizes the facets of organizing power, Garuda becomes the vehicle of this power. Wisnu is most commonly shown atop his winged mount, while Garuda carries the water of life, the *amerta*.

This embodiment of the Phoenix does not end in flames, but nonetheless bears much resemblance to other myths of its kind. This bird likewise possesses immortality and is an ally of the sun and fire. Garuda is the messenger of the gods, and in this way is much akin to Hermes. Like the Chinese Feng-huang, Garuda's responsibilities also focus on those of protecting and governing Wisnu's earthly kingdom. And similar to the bennu, Garuda is the bird that returns from the dark underworld bearing new life.

At Antioch, a colorful mosaic still exists which represents the Phoenix arising from the flames with solar rays encircling its head. In this instance, the Phoenix may be related to Roman mythology in the forms of Vulcan, the god of fire, and Vesta, the

## Three Myths

goddess of the hearth. Both these figures played principal roles in the Roman attitude toward fire. As a child, Vulcan, or in the Greek, Hephaestus, was thrown into the sea by his mother Hera because of a deformity. Once there, he was raised by two sea nymphs until he was old enough to learn a trade. Vulcan represents the properties of volcanic fire as well as the art of metalworkers, a skill at which he excelled. Vulcan was entrusted with fashioning the radiant gold helmet and breastplate of Helios, god of the Sun, and was married to Venus. It is also said that Prometheus acquired fire from Vulcan's workshop and brought it to earth. A great festival, known as Volcanalia, was held in his honor each year in Rome and Ostia. Since Dionysus and Vulcan had formed a close friendship, wine and excess were no doubt part of the festivities for hard-working Roman craftsmen of the anvil and fire.

Vulcan can also be directly linked with William Blake's solar figure of Los, the prophet of imagination. As a symbolic blacksmith of the inner nature of man, he is the mysterious inner fire, which transforms divine spirit into matter. His primary duty is to forge the barrier between the mortal soul and the land of eternal death. These responsibilities also correlate to the building of the walls of the legendary Judaic city Luz, described earlier. To the Roman people, the circular temple of Vesta was symbolic of the safety of their city. As long as the beacon of Vesta's fire could be seen, all was well. The ever-burning sacred flame was attended continually by six perfect vestal virgins who held an annual renewal of this sacred fire. The duties of these virgins were taken very seriously and infractions were punished severely. A vestal who broke her vows of chastity was buried alive and one who allowed the flame to die down was flogged. Sacrifices in this temple were prepared in Vesta's honor and burned to solicit continual favor from the Gods.

A similar focus on maintaining an eternal flame is also present in the Zoroastrian fire worship of the Parsee. Today in Iran, the Parsee continue to tend fires in their temples that have been burning for two thousand years. The Parsee utter all their sacred rituals in the presence of fire, which is considered the element of purification. By doing so, they intend to increase the

## Three Myths

power of good in the world and vanquish evil. The forces of good are championed by Ahura Mazda, while evil is represented by Ahriman. As foretold by the great prophet Zarathrusta (or Zoroaster), there is a constant struggle between the two, which leads to a pronounced apocalyptic aspect to his prophecies involving the final battle between the armies of Ahriman and Ahura Mazda. In his holy book, the *Avesta*, the world will be purged by molten metal, in which the righteous will wade as if through warm milk, and the evil will be incinerated. The purifying fire will then subside and return the world to a state of perfection. This tradition is repeated in the ordeals of the fire-walkers of southeast Asia who walk through roaring flames only to emerge completely unscathed. Such mastery over fire is said to be one of the true marks of holiness in some beliefs. There were also a number of clergy in 17th century England who held the same belief that the whole of humanity would be consumed in fire and arise from the flames renewed and purified. The strangest example of this was Solomon Eccles, a fanatical prophet of doom who would walk through the streets of London in the nude while bearing a burning cauldron on his head.

Infamous in Biblical scripture as a terrible deity to whom the Ammonites offered their firstborn, the Semitic god of fire, Molech (or Milcom) was another contemporary sacrificial effigy. The words of Leviticus 20:2-5 promise severe punishment to any Israelite or other group who worships Molech, by being stoned to death. In Jeremiah 32:35 Molech is associated with the sacrificial god Baal. The ancient priests of Baal were said to be required to eat the flesh of human sacrifices. Cahna-Baal, when translated, means the "Priests of Baal" and is very likely the origin of our modern word "cannibal." It was through Molech that the Canaanites worshipped the sun, that great fire of the heavens. Devotees to this idol would either pass their children between two fires or throw them through one in order to procure good fortune for their family and bountiful harvests. Molech is depicted as a massive bronze statue with the head of a bull and the body of a man. His name means "the lord of the altar of incense" and it is worth considering that there is a possible correspondence between the name Milcom and the Milchaum mentioned earlier. However, no distinctive record or image of

## Three Myths

the Phoenix concretely exists to verify this supposition. The great poet, John Milton refers to Moloch in Chapter 1 of his epic poem, *Paradise Lost*:

> First Moloch, horrid King besmear'd with blood
> Of human sacrifice, and parents tears,
> Though for the noyse of Drums and Timbrels loud
> Their childrens cries unheard, that past through fire
> To his grim Idol. Him, the Ammonite
> Worshipt in Rabba and her watry plain.

Some biblical scholars have ventured that Molech was none other than Yahweh and not a foreign deity worshipped in neighboring regions. Later Israelites were apparently so appalled by this practice of human sacrifice that they tried to blot out their shame by altering the name of the god from Yahweh to Molech. Whether or not this conscious adaptation is true, nevertheless it is strange behavior for a religion that received its divine commandments from a burning bush. At the beginning of 2nd Kings, the prophet Elijah commands this same divine fire to come down from heaven and kill a troop of one hundred soldiers that have come to capture him. While Elisha watches in the very next chapter, Elijah ascends to heaven in a flaming chariot, never to return to earth. To many UFOlogists, this is a favorite passage that demonstrates the classic scenario of an alien abduction. There certainly seems to be an unresolved question as to which deity truly holds command over fire. The Bible is rife with tales of flaming swords, tongues of fire, fire and brimstone, the glorious fire contained within the Ark of the Covenant, angels clothed in fire, heavenly wheels of fire, and finally the judgment of fire in Revelation. Like the *Avesta*, the Bible is so full of references to divine and apocalyptic flames, that one would almost expect the pages themselves to spontaneously combust. The fires of hell and heaven, it would seem, are not so much at odds with each other when they manifest as the same element. That is because this is the force of creative fire itself, which unites polarities. There is no good and evil because it is both. Just like the Milham, there is no reason to eat of the Tree of the Knowledge of Good and Evil once this is discovered because it encompasses and annihilates opposites. The Phoenix has already

## Three Myths

set up a roost in the highest branches of this Forbidden Tree. This is exactly the same manner in which the Alchemists depict the Phoenix. It is shown high atop the tree of alchemical process in a flaming nest. As the final stage of the operation for producing alchemical gold, the Phoenix is linked with *rubedo* (or reddening), just as it is also called Sol, the solar tincture. Shown in arcane diagrams as the final purifying and solidification phase of the *Lapis Philosophorum* or "great animal," the Phoenix holds great power. In his treatise, *A Subtle Allegory Concerning the Secrets of Alchemy*, Michael Maier, the great alchemist, speaks of a pilgrimage through the whole world with the goal of "discovering that wonderful bird the Phoenix." [8]

Maier sets out abroad in this alchemical fable on a trip throughout the continents of Europe, America, Asia, and Africa in hopes of locating the Phoenix. In his account, the Phoenix's flesh and feathers are said to be a glorious universal medicine for all passion, pain, and sorrow. After searching in vain in Europe, America, and Asia, Maier's quest finally draws him toward the Red Sea. There, he finds a virgin prophetess named the Erytheraen Sibyl living alone in a rocky cave. After reassuring her of his earnest longing to find the Phoenix, the Sibyl reveals that the Arabs and Egyptians have long rejoiced in the sole possession of the Phoenix. And though she cannot say exactly where the bird of legend is to be found, the Sibyl does give him several clues to finding the Phoenix. Her hints point Maier toward the seven mouths of the Nile, where he must search for Mercury (Hermes). Mercury has no fixed habitation and may be located at any one of the seven mouths at any time. So Maier is led on a wild Phoenix-chase across all seven mouths before retracing his steps and locating Mercury. Mercury shows him at great length where he must look for the Phoenix, but when Maier arrives at the designated place, the Phoenix has temporarily deserted its habitat to arbitrate a disagreement between the owl and other birds of the area. The Phoenix was not expected back for several weeks, and as Maier could not afford to wait, he ends his allegory by contenting himself with the information he has gained. But he determines to set out again at a future date to renew his search.

## Three Myths

Upon returning to his native land, Maier composed this epigram in honor of the Phoenix:

> "O Marvel of the World, prodigy without a blot, unique Phoenix who givest thyself to the great Sages! Thy feathers are red, and golden the hues of thy neck; thy nest is built of cassia and Saboean frankincense. When thy life is drawing to a close, thou knowest the secret way of Nature by which thou art restored to a new existence. Hence thou gladly placest thyself on the altar of Heliopolis, in order that Vulcan may give thee a new body. The golden glory of thy feathers is called the Medicine of health, and the cure of human woe. Thou has power to cast out disease and to make the old young again. Thee. Blessed Bird, I would rather have than all the wealth of the world, and the knowledge of thee was a delight which I sought for many years. Thou art hidden in the retreat of thine own nest, and if Pliny writes that he saw thee in Rome, he does greatly err. Thou art safe in thy home, unless some foolish boy disturb thee: if thou dost give thy feathers to anyone, I pray thee let him be a Sage."[9]

Around the same era as the golden age of alchemy, an astronomer named Johann Bayer published an astronomical catalogue of newly discovered constellations. A masterful work of art by any standards, the *Uranometria* was printed in 1603. It includes illustrated star maps that depict his revolutionary findings. Among the twelve new constellations he pinpointed is a constellation named Phoenix. This constellation is most prominently visible in the Southern Hemisphere, only in the months of winter. Interestingly, the Phoenix's position in the night sky relates to Alpha Canis Majoris, or Sirius. The sharp tail feathers of the Phoenix point, across the span of the night sky, directly at Sirius. As mentioned earlier, "Sirius" is derived from the Greek word for "scorching." In this particular stellar diagram, the Phoenix pictorially rises from the searing flames of the Dog Star. Every winter, the Phoenix flies from its flames and soars across the starry heavens to establish the boundary between the seasonal resuscitation and the departure of nature.

## Three Myths

In yet another mode of fire worship, bonfires were commonly used by the Celts in fire festivals that corresponded to the midpoints between seasonal solstice and equinox festivals. These bonfires burned on hilltops for three days, from sunset to sunset, rather than just sunset to sunrise. While the daytime hours maintained a mirthful carnival-like atmosphere, the evenings were usually reserved for the purpose of serious divination and, allegedly, human sacrifice. The four fire festivals are: Samhain (Nov.1) the Feast of the Dead, Imbolc or Candlemas (Feb. 1) the Return of Light, Beltane or May Day (May 1) the Fires of Bel (Baal), and Lughnasad (Aug. 1) the Feast of Lugh. In these ceremonies the immolation of sacrificial animals and in some cases, living humans was a regular practice, reportedly. The victims were commonly encased within woven wickerwork frames of branches and straw that were then ritually burnt to ashes and scattered on the soil to ensure fertility of crops and propagation of life. This custom may seem unusually cruel by modern standards, but in an agriculturally based civilization the bounty of harvest was considered foremost. From this age-old figure, the Wicker Man, we still retain its vestiges in the scarecrow, which is often seen on the outskirts of farmer's fields. To the Celtic people, who were inextricably bound to their land and its fruits, this method was justified by the simple necessity of the cycles of death and renewal demonstrated by Nature itself. The Phoenix also follows this same axiom of unbroken lifetimes. Without a real beginning or end, it is an immutable and eternal part of all Creation.

The notorious Hell-Fire Club of Dublin embraced a notably eccentric form of fire worship and revelry that shocked and scandalized the whole of 18th century England and Ireland. Among the aristocratic gentry of the time, there existed a small young group of men who devoted their every spare moment to gambling, whoring, blaspheming, and drinking. The clubs two

## Three Myths

founders were Richard Parsons, 1st Earl of Rosse, and Colonel Jack St.Leger, a descendant of three-time Governor of Ireland Sir Anthony St. Leger. Like his not too-distant relative, Jack St. Leger enjoyed large parties at his country house in county Kildare, which soon became the gathering place for drunken debauchery and gambling of large sums of money. It was in the intoxicating atmosphere of such parties that the Hell-Fire Club was first contrived. This beginning brings into focus a more infernal version of the Free Spirits. There are tales of the group drinking at a local tavern and dousing cats with raw Irish whiskey and setting them aflame to scare the crowds of would-be onlookers. When the screaming and flaming cat streaked out the door of the establishment, it was presumed that the Devil himself had appeared. This caused considerable panic and people trampled each other in the bedlam that followed.

The Dublin Hell-Fire Club's infamous reputation flourished over the next few years, though the real fun began after the Club took over a hunting lodge built high on Montpelier Hill, overlooking Dublin. For over twenty years, the group terrorized the surrounding area from its sinister perch and viciously took to all sorts of vice and blasphemy. The new principal figure in the Hell-Fire Club, Richard Chappell Whaley, a man who later emerged as holding a deep-seated hatred for religion in general and Catholicism in particular. This is ironic in view of his middle name. He made it a regular habit to amuse himself on Sundays by setting fire to the hedges and thatched roofs of the local Catholic chapels. A contemporary expression of pyromania has led to over two hundred church burnings and bombings in the U.S. since 1995. Whaley however, recanted after he saw a terrifying vision of Satan coming for him. He spent the last years of his life writing his memoirs on the Isle of Man, where he died of cirrhosis of the liver at age thirty-four. A new Hell-Fire Club has been founded in modern America as a decadent, semi-Satanic rock band called the Electric Hell-Fire Club. This group has not appropriated the Phoenix as their icon, but a Satanic folk-rock band called Changes from the early 1970's has. Changes was influenced by and involved with the Process Church of the Final Judgement, a Scientological cult whose members became famous for wearing black cloaks and selling their lavish, eponymous magazines. In the issue devoted to the subject of death, R. N. Taylor, one of the founders of Changes, contributed a psychedelic drawing of a Phoenix bursting out of a skull-shaped planet. This illustration now appears on the cover of the recently released Changes CD, which has a song called, "Fire of Life."

The sacrificial element of fire worship recurs in almost every religion throughout the world. From the fire worship of the Aztecs to the Zoroastrians, a common thread is shared in their veneration of holy fire and its association to a common solar constituent. The Hindu god of fire, Agni is seen as having red horses and flaming hair, representing both a solar element and sacrificial fire form. *Agni* is thus easily related to the Greek god, *Vulcan*. In early South American civilization, as well, we see early versions of the Phoenix. In the Aztec religion it takes the shape of Quetzalcoatl, the Feathered Serpent, God of the Wind, which suggests that this flying serpent likewise sailed across the sky; accompanying the sun on its daily trek from horizon to horizon. When portrayed as the plumed serpent, Quetzal, this deity symbolized the blending of heaven and earth. He was also addressed as Master of Life, since he brought great prosperity and knowledge to his people. Like Prometheus, he gave the myth-believing Mesoamericans the gift of fire. Quetzalcoatl is often described as an undulating serpent with shimmering multi-colored scales and bright feathers around its neck and head. This image reminds us of the fire serpent of Tantra. Quetzalcoatl's main temple at Tenochtitlan was built with circular walls because it was believed they offered no sharp obstacles to the god of the wind. It was Quetzalcoatl who was wrongly expelled from his lofty homeland by the jealous Sun God, Tetzcatlipoca. Quetzalcoatl then wandered down the coast of South America to the shores of the Atlantic Ocean where he immolated himself on a pyre and emerged in the heavens as the bright planet Venus. The main temple of Quetzalcoatl's cult is located in Cholula, Mexico. There one can see the beautiful gargoyle heads of Quetzalcoatl, as the feathered serpent, decorating the stone pyramid.

The fiery self-destruction of the Phoenix is echoed in the ritual of cremation. Fire is renowned worldwide as a purifying ele-

## Three Myths

ment that burns away the dross of the spirit, leaving it refined and closer to God. Fire always reaches toward the heavens and is thought to be a fitting way to speed the soul on its way to the other world. Mystically, the soul leaves the physical body as a flame rising up through the crown of the head. With cremation, the earthly body is consumed in a sea of flames, while the soul is conveyed aloft as smoke back to its Source. Permanent scaffolds for cremation of the dead are placed near the Ganges River in India, where the ashes may be committed to the waters while prayers are offered. In Bali, when a king dies, the villagers carry his body to an elaborately constructed tower, where he is placed together with effigies of Garuda and other animals and burnt. Burning on the funeral pyre is an accepted custom in many parts of the world as an efficient method of disposing of corpses. The only religions that seem to take exception are Zoroastrianism and Judaism. As far back as during the period of the Black Plague, cremation was recommended by Nostradamus, a medical student and prophetic seer, as the best method for curbing the spread of the disease. Christianity too, at one time objected to cremation because it seemed to invalidate the doctrine of the resurrection of the body. As we have already seen, this dilemma was resolved by the introduction of the Phoenix into their system of belief. It has also been the practice in Hindu parts of India for the bereaved widow to throw herself on to her husband's funeral pyre and be consumed by the same flames that burn up his remains. This bizarre religious belief is called *suttee* or *sati* and still occurs with some frequency, though it was made illegal during the time of British colonial rule in India. Sati is the name of the consort of the Hindu god of destruction, Shiva, who was humiliated by her father, King Daksha. Because of Daksha's anger against her husband, she burned herself to death. This mythology has passed on what amounts to a type of emotional blackmail that gives women a sense of self-glorification, but with deadly results.

In this century, self-combustion has become a prevalent form of political protest around the world, as well as an expression of grief. Between 1932-33, in one region of the Urals in Russia, more than one thousand Old Believer monks and nuns committed suicide by self-immolation or drowning. The Old Believ-

*Three Myths*

ers were a holdout sect that did not agree to reform with the rest of the Russian Orthodox Church, which subsequently persecuted the Old Believers who were despised as heretics. In 1965, a man in Tamil Nadu, India burnt himself to death in protest against the government's effort to impose Hindi as the native language. In 1987, about thirty people died from self-immolating in grief at the death of Tamil Nadu's Chief Minister, a former matinee idol. In 1990, several high caste students, including women, died in self-imposed flames to protest a government ruling to reserve more state jobs for lower caste applicants. In 1991, after the Gulf War in Kuwait, the uncontrolled fiery spouts of 628 burning oil wells could be seen writhing day and night for almost a year. The landscape could only be described in the terms of a small-scale Armageddon, just as ecologically terrible as the one in the book of Revelation. In February of 1994, Dr. Homa Darabi of Tehran, Iran, drove to a local square on the tenth day of Ramadan, emptied a can of gasoline on her head, and began shouting at the top of her lungs, "Death to oppression! Long live liberty!" Then, she lit a match and died in a blaze so extreme that passersby could not put it out in time. It later became known that she had lost her job at a health clinic where she worked for refusing to wear the traditional Islamic dress to work. In another part of Iran on the same day that Dr. Darabi wantonly committed suicide, a 14-year-old girl set fire to herself to escape a forced marriage with a 44-year-old man. As recently as November 1996, activists from the Forum to Awaken Women declared that one member of its group would stage a human torch protest on each of the seventeen days leading up to the Miss World Pageant in Bangalore, India. The militant traditionalist group stated that the contest was "an affront to both women and the culture in India." [10] It would seem that F.A.W. is fighting one offense to women's lives with a greater one; that of suttee. Even the local Farmers Association threatened to torch the cricket stadium where the event was being held. In the end, only one 25-year-old tailor some 200 miles away, who was a member of a youth branch of the Communist Party, set himself on fire.

In Western theater, something akin to suttee is portrayed in the climactic conclusion of Richard Wagner's opera, *Gotterdammerung*. In order to restore Nature's equilibrium and

## Three Myths

lift the curse that lies on the Ring of the Niebelung, Brunnhilde, the Valkyrie heroine must return the hexed gold to the Rhine. She accomplishes this, and in a Phoenix-like act of self-immolation she flings herself upon the funeral pyre of her husband, Siegfried. The Valkyries in Norse mythology are sometimes depicted as beautiful winged women who carry the fallen heroes of battle to Valhalla and their greater glory. Here again, throwing oneself into the fire is cast in a macabre, lambent light as a noble and supreme self-sacrifice.

One of this century's most memorable incidents of self-inflammation was captured by photographer Malcolme Browne in Saigon in 1963. Thich Quang Duc, a monk of the United Buddhist Church of Vietnam, touched off a volatile one-man protest that sent a stark message of the intolerable situation in his country. After quietly finding a clearly visible spot in a public street, Quang Duc doused his orange robes with gasoline, assumed the meditation pose of the Buddha, and set himself ablaze. This demonstration yielded strong reactions from both sides of the Vietnam War. Some see Qang Duc's fiery suicide as a pivotal moment in the toppling of the Dien government. The photo of this flaming monk was published in *Life* magazine and was accordingly seen all over the world within days after it happened.

This particular form of Buddhism is called *Mahayana*, which differs from other sects in its attitude toward encouraging suicide for religious motives. The Lotus Sutra praises the burning of one's body as the "highest offering," like a sort of human incense stick. Mahayana's peculiar Buddhist order views this kind of ascetic self-surrender as a method of attaining virtue in the next reincarnated life. Is this some long-forgotten subconscious mimetic of the Phoenix, or just wishful self-delusion? However this strange self-inflicted pyromania is explained, it is typified in all cases by a frenzied excess of veneration that overrides the inhibitions of the flesh. Carried to the extreme, the devotees find positive pleasure in their sacrifice. This furor is a way of expressing the degree of their loyalty to the divinity they worship, be it a certain political ideal or a deity. Mahayana's doctrine of self-immolation for karmic gain is perceived by other Buddhist groups as aberrant. In the Great Discourse by Buddha

## Three Myths

on the Lion's Roar verse 61, he says, "there are certain recluses and Brahmins whose doctrine and view is this: 'Purification comes about through fire worship.' But it is impossible to find a kind of fire that has not already been worshipped by me in this long journey, when I was either a head-anointed noble king or a well-to-do Brahmin." For Buddhists everywhere, these are indeed words to live by.

The Statue of Liberty holds a flaming torch that corresponds to the revered eternal flame of the ancients. But for some apocalyptic groups this flame symbolizes not liberty, but liberation. Since the early part of 1993 the news media has incessantly covered the activities of various small, but well-organized, upstart "cults." These groups have been labeled "doomsday cults," not only for their constant obsessional belief that the end of the world is nigh, but also because some have armed themselves with large caches of weapons. As such, they form a human barrier against the FBI and other federal agencies. Such is the tragic self-fulfilling prophecy of the Branch Davidians that began in late February of 1993 in Waco, Texas. Their leader, David Koresh, sang his own amateur brand of rock tunes, while claiming to be the reincarnation of Christ. Koresh espoused biblical passages from Matthew chapter 24, which is a sermon by Jesus on the prophetic destruction of the temple in Jerusalem and the coming end times. He effectively used these scriptures to reinforce his apocalyptic views in the imaginations of his followers. Many other of these so-called cults also predictably share a great passion for the book of Revelations.

The ATF was called in to investigate the stockpiling of illegal weapons by the Davidians, and were greeted by gunfire. Over the fifty-one day standoff that followed, an unparalleled blitz of news coverage had the nation, and indeed the world, watching as local Waco and federal lawmen descended upon the Mt. Carmel compound. Inside the small cluster of buildings, around one hundred men, women, and children dug in and prepared for Armageddon. Their notions, that these were the end times, were quickly confirmed as ATF and FBI agents brought in a small militia of tanks and soldiers to surround the cult members inside. Finally on April the 19th, FBI tanks moved in as batter-

*Three Myths*

ing rams and punctured the side of the main building to allegedly pump tear gas into the facility. Shortly thereafter, flames erupted around the perimeter of the buildings. And within minutes, the entire Davidian compound was consumed in a large volcanic blast of flame, punctuated by an unexplained explosion. The ensuing conflagration left no doubt what would be found in the flaming rubble. In all, approximately eighty-two bodies were found, twenty of them children. Most corpses were charred beyond recognition and, in some cases, identification was impossible. The epilogue of news stories that followed would like for us believe that the fire was the result of an intentional murder/suicide by fire of the Davidians, but this supposition remains unproved. Fire destroys evidence more efficiently than any other method of concealment, and many doubts have been cast upon the methods and testimony of law enforcement officials involved in the raid on Mt. Carmel.

As another example, the Order of the Solar Temple is viewed with much the same suspicion as the Koreshites in Waco. Their fire-related deaths, or "departures" as they are known within the cult, have recently reached a total of seventy-four members and their children. On October 11, 1994, in a bizarre coordinated murder/suicide across two continents, fifty-three Solar Temple members and their children died in separate calculated rituals that ended in flames. The charismatic lecturer and founder of the Solar Temple, Luc Jouret, was quick to dispense his prophecies of environmental catastrophes that would engulf all the earth, excepting only an elected few. He also loved to talk about the transformative power of fire. On a Swiss radio broadcast in 1987, Jouret said, "we are in a reign of fire, everything is being consumed." [11] Already, signs of the Phoenix began to loom in Jouret's cold-blooded scheme. Luc Jouret was fascinated by the early 14th century mystic Knights Templar, and in 1981 he assumed the leadership of the Reformed Catholicism, formerly run by ex-Gestapo man Julien Orgias. Adopting Catholic rituals of communion and mass during which he acted as priest, in 1984 Jouret set up his own group, the Order of the Solar Temple, or Temple Solaire. He used this pseudo-religion as a platform for his lectures which included everything from homeopathic healing to his own apocalyptic perspectives on the destruction

## Three Myths

of the world. Eventually, he gathered enough followers to form a core group and began urging them to collect arsenals of weapons in preparation for the end of the world. Most of the people involved in this inner circle of the O.S.T. in every external appearance led normal lives, until the veneer was burnt away and the horrible truth was revealed in 1994.

The first grim incident was reported, around midnight on the night of October 11, by concerned neighbors who saw flames issuing from a nearby farmhouse. When firemen arrived at the cottage in Chiery, Switzerland, that belonged to Albert Giacobino, they found an odd cassette tacked to the door. The audio cassette, when played, contained a rambling demented speech about coming natural disasters and the occurrence of astronomical alignments. The partially burned interior of the cabin contained, not only the robed bodies of twenty-two dead Solar Temple members, but also an elaborately mirrored temple room with red satin curtains. The corpses were found arranged in a circular sunburst pattern on the floor of the temple facing up toward a Christlike portrait of their mentor, Luc Jouret. Most had been shot in the head, and ten had plastic bags tied over their heads. Some of the deceased had been heavily drugged. As if in a final celebration, the floor of the room was littered with empty champagne bottles. A few hours later and fifty miles away, in Granges-sur-Salvan, the charred bodies of twenty-five more Solar Temple members were found arranged and executed in a similar fashion. Among the bodies was one identified as Luc Jouret. Apparently, the fires that engulfed both houses had been detonated using a rigged system of electrical wires running from telephones into containers of highly flammable material. These diabolical mechanisms were set to trigger the ignition of the firebombs from a remote source by a simple phone call. Perhaps this cremation of the bodies was intended to speed the souls' journey to Sirius, their supposed destination. But more than likely, it was again a fire used to obliterate evidence of the murders.

Across the Atlantic in Morin Heights, Canada, at about the same time, police were investigating the smoldering rubble of a house belonging to Joseph Di Mambro, one of the leaders of the Solar Temple in Canada. Another five burnt bodies were discovered,

## Three Myths

including a 3-month-old baby boy. Of the other bodies found, two wore red and gold medallions bearing a double-headed eagle with the letters T.S., for Temple Solaire. One of these was identified as Joseph Di Mambro. It later turned out that another two adults were the baby's parents. Like their infant son, they were ritually stabbed to death before the fire was ever set. The irrational motivation for their murders was later revealed to have been due to an internal religious dispute between Di Mambro and the parents of the child. Di Mambro as leader, had announced during his ceremonies that he had not only been a member of the Knights Templar in a previous lifetime, but also that his daughter Emanuelle was a "cosmic child" that had been produced without sex. In these ceremonies, the members wore Crusade-type robes and were allowed to hold a sword that Di Mambro claimed had been given to him one thousand years ago. Shortly after this, when a couple in the cult gave birth to a baby boy, they named their own son Emmanuel. This angered Di Mambro and he vehemently proclaimed the child as the Antichrist and ordered the cold-blooded ceremonial murder of the entire family. After the initial shock of these weird murder/suicides, the Solar Temple cult slowly faded from public attention.

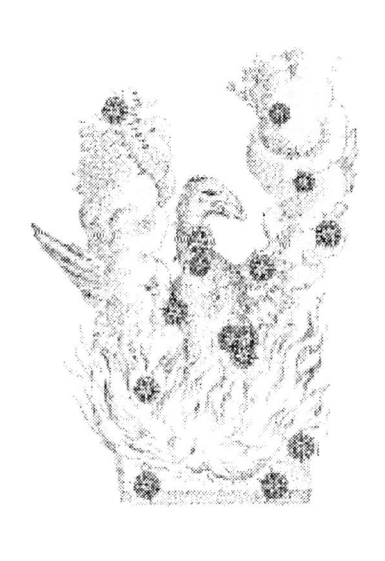

Then in late December of 1995, in the forested region of Grenoble, France sixteen more bodies of Solar Temple members burned. Like the previous incidents, the pattern of murder/suicide was repeated. The bodies were again arranged in a circle, and some had plastic bags tied over their heads. Most had taken a deadly mixture of toxic chemicals and sedatives before being shot point blank in the head and set on fire. Among the dead identified were two French policemen, Patrick Vuarnet, son of a French skiing champion, the wife of one policeman, and three children of cult members aged two, four, and six years. The bullets positively identified the guns of the policemen as the murder weapons. After investigation it was concluded that the policemen had assisted in the other suicides and then shot and incinerated the bodies, then shot themselves. There is still some suspicion that other Solar Temple members were present and fled after the deaths. The number of dead cult members soared to sixty-nine. Again, Luc Jouret's words seemed to hover over the gruesome scene: "Liberation is not where human beings think it is. Death can be an essential stage of life." These words allude to the cult's conceptual "journey" through death to their reincarnated lives on a "planet" known as Sirius. The latest lethal incident involving the Solar Temple was a mass suicide of five members at house in St. Casimir, Quebec. This event that occurred on March 23, 1997, brings the fiery death toll of the group to seventy-four.

The Order of the Solar Temple's activities are linked to the Phoenix by several points. Joseph Di Mambro's daughter, Emanuelle, was supposedly conceived without sexual reproduction; much like the method of the Phoenix. Although no mention is made of how Emanuelle was born, fire was considered to be the cult's primary symbol of death and rebirth. The solar element is directly connected with the Phoenix, as is the method of blazing deaths that followers used to translate the murdered members to the afterlife. Luc Jouret's belief in rebirth through fire was undoubtedly inspired by the Phoenix. Since he had been a member of a Catholic organization, he was probably aware of the Phoenix as the symbolic doctrine of Christ's resurrection. The Solar Templars also had a predominant belief in reincarnation on a faraway planet called Sirius. At least in name, this seems to indicate a knowledge of the Sothic cycle that was encoded by the Egyptians in the Phoenix myth. All of the original fifty-three who died, including Jouret and Di Mambro, made an initiation trip to Egypt a few years before their deaths. Furthermore, Di Mambro claimed that he was a reincarnated Templar Knight who was chosen to guide the members through death and to the planet Sirius. There is almost certainly a connection here with the Egyptian Book of the Dead, in which the bennu plays such an important role in guiding the soul through the

## Three Myths

land of death. Jouret was also obsessed with the legends of the Knights Templar, a heretical group of Crusaders that sprang up in Germany and France about the same time period as the Brethren of the Free Spirit. Members of the Templars, the Free Spirits, and possibly even the Sect of the Phoenix were tried and burned at the stake during the Inquisition for allegedly practicing heretical sexual rites.

Another possible Phoenix connection exists in the months shortly before October 1994. Luc Jouret had at one time approached the Australian aborigines about holding a Solar Temple ceremony at Ayers Rock in Australia. Ayers Rock is a site held sacred by the Australian aborigines. It is also the center of their "dreamtime" mythology and the dwelling place of their gods. There have been continual land disputes over Ayers ever since this outcropping of rock was identified as the largest known deposit of uranium in the Southern Hemisphere. Jouret's request for access to Ayers Rock was denied and the land remains, at least for now, in the care of the aboriginals. Because Ayers is in an elevated and remote portion of the southern part of the globe, it is also an ideal spot for viewing the Phoenix constellation. Late in the month of October, the Phoenix would have been clearly visible in the night sky from atop Ayers Rock. Although no overt connection to the Phoenix is present, the circumstances and philosophy behind the Solar Temple are sufficient to suggest the underlying archetype.

Presently, new incarnations of Phoenix behavior may be just beath the surface of civilization, waiting to flare up again. We must be very cautious not to stand too close to this Phoenix when its impulse takes over. Otherwise, the blaze that it uses to renew itself may scald the globe. Within its throes of rebirth, a new Phoenix must be nurtured that will embody a greater respect for life's precious gifts. As Carl Jung writes in his book, *The Psychology of the Child Archetype*:

Archetypes were, and still are, living psychic forces that demand to be taken seriously, and they have a strange way of making sure of their effect. Always they were the bringers of protection and salvation, and their violation has as its consequence the 'perils of the soul' known to us from the psychology of primitives. Moreover, they are the infallible causes of neurotic and even psychotic disorders, behaving exactly like neglected or maltreated physical organs or organic functional systems. [12]

With the recent suicides of Solar Temple members fresh in our collective consciousness, as the new millennium draws near we can expect to see even more incomprehensible behavior involving arson and fire-related prophecies. Using the Bible as their touchstone, just about any fundamentalist Christian group likely believes that the world will end in fire. From cults that harbor self-fulfilling apocalypse to the door-to-door rantings of Armageddon by Jehovah's Witnesses, the possibilities abound. We seem surrounded by various groups that each have their own convincing interpretation of the end times. Even the Internet, a supposed tool of freedom for communication, has become a seductive manipulation of our viewpoints. By accepting the simulacrum on the screen as fact, we are being tricked and deceived by the mechanisms of our own imaginations. Encapsulated fantasies overflow from this realm of burgeoning information and seep into our everyday perceptions of the world outside. The timeless myths that have instructed and rejuvenated our societies run the risk of being reinterpreted in dangerous and impersonal ways. Our expectations of the future and recollections of the past are, in some means, being homogenized by this disembodied sea of data. This same characteristic of standardized thought or dogma among its members is part of what classifies a "cult" as such. Perhaps this is why the Heaven's Gate cult chose to post their fabrications on the Internet. In this immaterial form, there is no frame of reference from the outside world to hold against it. It also rekindles a certain feeling about liberation from the physical body, about moving into a kind of virtual fantasy land. We are encouraged to take a voyeuristic peek through the keyhole with only death staring back at us and promising paradise.

Most people feel a certain amount of anxiety that something of great importance is about to surface at the millennial marker. It has always been part of our human nature to seek and identify patterns in the events and objects around us. But only by mistaking these patterns, or mythologies, for reality do we become susceptible to their control over us. There is a natural tendency to believe that somehow we are involved in a significant, but undefined historic event. Perhaps it is true, but we must also keep in mind our infinite abilities for self-deception. It is unfortunate that the outlook seems filled with only fear and trepidation. Christian groups reinforce this sense of doom by becoming more militant in their tactics and more intolerant toward other's views. A topical example of how ludicrous this stance has become is the boycotting of Disney World by Southern Baptists. Like the "cults," they seek to create a schism between themselves and the rest of society. By assuming this type of antagonistic position, they only add fuel to the flames. They feel that their unyielding belief alone will insulate them from impending worldly disasters. This is one of the most dangerous forms of fatalist doctrine. It leads directly to both prejudice and apathy for our growing problems as humans on this planet. With so many religious groups believing in divine deliverance from their worldly problems, they feel no need to resolve the very things that threaten to bring about our destruction. In fact, millennial groups seek the world's destruction expectantly. The Phoenix could be regarded in this context as an allusion to the increasing threat of global warming. And yet, there is no more reason for faith in divine deliverance than there is for believing the Phoenix really does physically exist. It is pure mythology. Conveyed through the long annals of history, these fictions exist almost entirely in our minds. It is how we choose to utilize our self created myths that will make the difference between a prospect of calamity or rebirth.

One thing seems evident, the greater the intolerance to variety and innovation in culture, the more the roaring fires are fanned. It may not be just the doomsday cults that will enter the flames next time. The apprehensive and suspicious gaze of the nation is now directed inward at its own citizens. There is a new enemy and it appears as ourselves. Our military forces are goaded into domestic situations similar to those they used to face overseas. In this way, the great American Eagle has the potential to become a stygian variant of the Phoenix — caught between the bright hope of Western civilization and the explosive inner turmoil that threatens to consume the whole world. Its wings take

## Three Myths

on the shape of a stealth bomber, and its talons no longer clutch the olive branch of peace and arrows of defense. Instead they wield an immense nuclear fireball. This must not be so. We must master our myths, or they will master us. Our greatest challenge is to make sure the Inquisitions of the last millennium are left there. But in some ways, we still persist in utilizing the same mindset as our distant ancestors did. Perpetuated through the last one thousand years, this trend has become an inherent habit. We must churn up these murky waters in order to retrieve the vital undercurrents of our models of the world. Small islands and eruptions of forgotten insight occasionally break on e surface of the present by their own accord in unexpected ways. But like colossal volcanoes, they appear across the oceans of history, then cool and sink again back into the depths. For the most part we see only the floatsam of our limited knowledge through the lens of history and doctrine bobbing upon the filmy surface. These restrictive viewpoints are often held up against a changing world to which they no longer belong. This often results in a wedge of misanthropy being driven into our relations with one another. In turn, this alienation proves to be the fertile ground that allows dangerous "cults" to flourish. Perhaps their disillusion stems from misunderstanding their own archetypes, as pointed out by Jung. In this case, a Phoenix that does not wish to be reborn is no longer the legendary symbol of willful renewal, but only a species bent on suicide. The expanse of death is indeed real and absolute, but where do we go from nowhere? This seems to be an instance of *ex nihilo, nihil fit*, which means *from nothing, comes nothing*. The destiny of our world cannot emerge into the next millennium through the continuation of reckless self-destructive imitation of that which has gone before. Progress only comes by clearing away those obsolete ideas that would inhibit us from fulfilling our true purpose.

In some ways, the Phoenix serves as our lasting symbol of struggle to grasp those strange impenetrable mysteries of life and death and enfold them within a poetic fire of allegory. Such perplexing questions of from whence we came and where we are going are, probably, the impetus for the initial invention of the mythical Phoenix. As the world changes, this question re-

*Three Myths*

veals itself in new permutations and it deepens in significance at the same time. The old Phoenix has been consumed in the conflagration of late twentieth century violence, while the first duty of the newly arisen manifestation should be to put the ashes of its predecessor to rest and to begin anew. By inflaming our hearts with the passionate purusit of reviving basic humanity, we stand poised on the verge of an endless vista of potentiality. Once this prospect is approached, it can provide valuable methods from which to improve upon our past. This reborn Phoenix must also shape its own possibilities, unfettered by previous incarnations. The cycle of the Phoenix is striving to teach us about new beginnings, new aeons. Even the Phoenix must eventually transform itself. The wafting spices of Nature's nest beckon us from the wildernesses of our forgotten past. Its scents drift through our memories and rejuvenate our collective longing for humanity. The bright sun of desire ignites the imaginations of those who dare to burn with such loving intensity. From out of the abstract shapes that dance in the lambent flames of the spirit, the shape of the Phoenix rematerializes. Only by pursuing our greatest dreams will the Phoenix within our purest aspirations be able to arise from its ashes.

**ACKNOWLEDGEMENTS**

A great BIG Thank You to my beloved wife, Sandra for her patience and help with the wonderful illustrations. Kudos to Rodney Perkins for his persistence in hammering this book into shape and to Philip Walker for his cover layout. My gratitude to Chris Dolan of Washburn Observatory for clarifying information on the Phoenix constellation. My Thanks also to Jason Cohen for his continued encouragement and support and to Steve Holland for beginning a new Cycle.

## Three Myths

**ENDNOTES**

[1] Barber, Richard: *Man, Myth and Magic*, Volume 16, pg.2185 BPC Publishing Ltd., 1970

[2] Grant, Kenneth: *Cults of the Shadow*, pg.54   Samuel Weiser, 1976

[3] Budge, Sir Wallis, translator: *The Egyptian Book of the Dead*, pg.552   Carol Publishing Group, 1994

[4] Ibid, pg.379

[5] Lerner, Robert: *The Heresy of the Free Spirit in the Later Middle Ages*, pg.11   University of Notre Dame Press, 1972

[6] Kraig, Donald Michael: *Modern Magick*, pg. 433   Llewellyn Publications, 1988

[7] Lerner, Robert: *The Heresy of the Free Spirit in the Later Middle Ages*, pg.75   University of Notre Dame Press, 1972

[8] Roob, Alexander: *Alchemy and Mysticism*, pg.695   Benedikt Taschen Verlag, 1997

[9] Maier, Michael:   *A Subtle Allegory Concerning the Secrets of Alchemy*, Book 12 of Symbola Aureae Mensae Duodccim Nationum, Frankfurt, 1617.

[10] *Indo-American News/* October 1996

[11] Lacayo, Richard: *Cults: In the Reign of Fire*, Time Magazine/ October 17, 1994

[12] Jung, Carl: *The Psychology of the Child Archetype*. Part I: The Archetypes and the Collective Unconscious., 1940

BAPHOMET

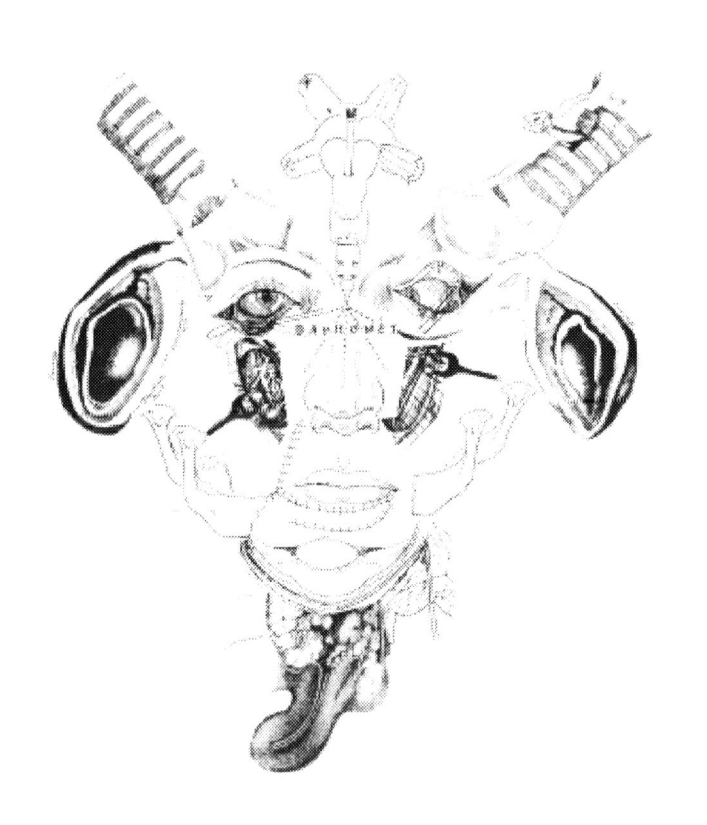

# The Baphomet in History and Symbolism
## by Forrest Jackson

Before embarking upon the historical examination of the enigmatic figure of the Baphomet, the androgynous goat-headed god of the Templars and the present-day symbol of Satanism, I must tell of my introduction to the bestial god. When I was a child, I was somewhat sickly, so one day while in the third grade (1980), I stayed home from school. As was my habit at the time, I scanned through the TV channels in search of something decent worth watching — not an easy task when considering the preponderance of inane programming. After flipping past *Gilligan's Island* and worse fare, I finally settled on a rare, diurnal horror movie broadcast.

Though I can barely recall it through the cob-webbed corridors of my labyrinthine memories, I think that I can do some justice to the plot. There was a young couple (perhaps newlyweds) who traveled through a strange town set in either England or New England. Each citizen of this town walked with a limp, which was a happenstance of great mystery to the travelers in the TV set and to me on the couch, lying feverishly afraid. Eventually, the heroine was pinioned to a Satanic altar, above which the Baphomet was pentagonally represented. Just before she was to be sacrificed by a cult of these limping creeps, the secret of the maladjusted legs was revealed — along with a normal appendage, everyone had one goat leg, complete with cloven hoof. The heresiarch presiding over the sacrifice modestly lifted the skirt of the imperiled lady and she, too, had developed a goat leg.

For some reason, this bestial transplantation produced a mental enjambment in me which runs on to the present day. I walked, or limped, away from this experience a changed kid and I distinctly remember drawing an extremely Satanic sketch of a goat-head in a pentagram. I was frightened by this drawing, so I hid it from my teacher (a mundanely evil Ms. Drake) and my parents. So, though it is thoroughly typical that a mere movie would so greatly affect me as a child, this particular film led to my lifelong obsession with evil, the bestial, and the occult. At this point I should say that I am not a practicing Satanist, but I do love the goat more so than the lamb.

## THE HISTORY OF THE KNIGHTS TEMPLAR

In order to understand the history of the Baphomet and its diabolical significance, we must study the origin, accusations of blasphemy, and subsequent myths of the Knights Templar, for it is they who invented the Baphomet. Hailing from the southwestern region of France, Hugues de Payen and eight other men founded the monastic knighthood in 1118 AD for the purpose of protecting pilgrims heading to the Holy Land. Along with vows of chastity, poverty, and obedience, the Knights swore to fight Mohammed's troops and to secure the city of Jerusalem for the cause of Christ, or at least for the causes of deadly zealous Christians sitting on thrones, both royal and papal, in Western Europe. The first Crusade was considered successful, but the second one ended in a Christian loss from which the Church never recovered. In 1187, when the Templars lost the "True Cross" during the battle of the Horns of Hattin and later surrendered Jerusalem to the armies of Saladin, there was no longer justification for the preservation of their Order.

However, throughout their existence the Templars had become fabulously rich, so they continued to operate until the 14th century. Previous to their aforementioned defeat, Innocent II vouchsafed them a papal Bull, or proclamation, in 1139 called *Omne Datum Optimum*, which means "every best gift" in Latin. This gift meant that the Templars were a sovereignty unto themselves and were accountable only to the Pope. They reserved

## Three Myths

the freedom to elect their own masters and chaplains and the right to keep any booty they could wrest from the Saracens. Just as importantly, the monk-knights were freed from paying rents and tithes and were granted the capacity to collect such taxes. Because both ecclesiastical and noble institutions trusted them, the Order acted as an international bank, in which function they invented check-writing and loans, despite potential charges of usury and avarice. In 1185, the London Temple protected the deposits of the royal treasure.[1] It is precisely due to the wealth they accrued that the Order was officially suppressed in 1307 by Pope Clement V. This suppression led to the confessions of blasphemy and pagan worship of the Baphomet, both of which eventuated in their dissolution.

Philip the Fair, the wrongly christened King of France, had once sought to join the Templars, but was refused. This rejection turned him against the Order that had once protected him from a revolt. So, under the ruse of mustering troops for a new crusade, he suggested that the Templars and Hospitaliers (who were rivals) should consolidate. Through this arrangement, Philip hoped to acquire much of the spare wealth, estates, and castles of the knights. The union never occurred, but the king soon succeeded in spreading rumors of misconduct about the rich monks.

"The method by which the charges were originally said to have been made was through a former Templar who had been expelled from the Order for heresy and other offenses. This Squin de Flexian found himself in prison with another man (a Florentine named Notto Dei) and they thought they could obtain their release for the crime of which they were currently accused if they would testify against the Order."[2] As is evident, the original charges (some of which are summarized below) arose from the felonious desperation of one or two men who did not tell the absolute truth; hardly a credible manner in which to assign blame to the Order. The most serious accusations were that the Templars:

- had secret alliances with the Saracens,
- spat and trampled upon the cross,
- murdered initiates and knights who wished to leave the order,
- killed children, perhaps ritualistically, and instructed women to perform abortions,
- had perverted sexual practices,
- and held any action committed for the betterment of the Order to be above sin.

Then on 12 August, 1308, extended complaints were issued against the Order. Of the 127 repetitive items, only about a dozen correspond to charges of idolatry. Though not named so at the time, the Baphomet's blasphemous worship by the Templars was detailed in the following translation:

- that in each province they had idols, namely heads, of which some had three faces, and some one, and others had a human skull.
- that they adored these idols or that idol, and especially in their great chapters and assemblies.
- that they venerated [them].
- that [they venerated them] as God.
- that [they venerated them] as their Saviour.
- that some of them [did].
- that the majority of those who were in the chapters [did].
- that they said that that head could save them.
- that [it could] make riches.
- that it gave them all the riches of the Order.
- that it made the trees flower.
- that [it made] the land germinate.
- that they surrounded or touched each head of the aforesaid idols with small cords which they wore around themselves next to the shirt or the flesh.
- that in his reception, the aforesaid small cords or some lengths of them were given to each of the brothers.
- that they did this in adoration of an idol.

The document uses Christian terminology (like "Saviour") in accusation of paganism; specifically, of the ancient mystical variety. The suggestion that the worship of the head caused the land to germinate brings to mind pre-Christian fertility ceremonies, which were considered witchcraft by the Church. So, though most Templars thought of themselves as devoutly Catholic knights, there is some evidence in the confessions that an inner order of Templars indeed followed pagan practices. Regarding the rejection of Christ, one knight named Fulk de Troyes claimed that during his initiation, his conductor showed him a crucifix and said, "set not much faith in this, for it is too young."[3]

It is true that — when tortured and interrogated — several knights confessed to being sodomites in addition to acting contrary to Catholic doctrine, but only twelve spoke of the worship of a head. Sometimes called Baphomet, this head was "variously described as an androgynous deity with two faces and a long white beard, or a human skull, which uttered oracular prophecies and guided the Order. Some writers on the Templars have even speculated that this image was the Turin shroud, allegedly the garment used to wrap the body of Jesus after his death."[4] The validity of the accusations are extremely suspicious, however, because the list also propounds the unlikely theory that the Templars worshipped a common housecat.

The charge that the Templars maintained a secret pact with the Saracens is an allegation that may be rooted in fact, which helps to explain the myth of the Head's prophecy. Although the Christians and Muslims were at war, occasionally alliances were made. Notably, the Ismaelian Assassins in Syria were infamous for their wavering sense of patriotism. They and the Templars independently fought Saladin's troops, so it is likely that the two secret societies met favorably on equal grounds. The Templars may have learned much from the Assassins. Joseph von Hammer-Purgstall alleges that "the Ismaelians (Assassins) was [sic] the original, and the Order of the Templars, the copy."[5] Indeed both armies wore red and white, but Hammer-Purgstall, was neither an objective nor dispassionate historian, basing his questionable evidence for the pagan worship of the Baphomet on shards of pottery and the Grail legend. And, the Assassins worshipped their Master, The Old Man of the Mountains — not the Baphomet. Whatever the case, the accusation that the Templars regularly cried out "Ya Allah!" was surely damning testimony for the Order, whether it was true or not.

Although Catholics of the time (and for centuries later) were eager to suspect that Baphomet was a French corruption of Mahomet, which is another name for Mohammed, this transliterative correlation may not be valid. Idries Shah, in his informative book about Sufism, says that:

> Probably relying upon contemporary Eastern sources, Western scholars have recently supposed that "Bafomet" has no connection with Mohammed, but could well be a corruption of the Arabic *abufihamat* (pronounced in the Moorish Spanish something like *bufihimat*). The word means "father of understanding." In Arabic, "father" is taken to mean "source, chief seat of," and so on. In Sufi terminology, *ras el-fahmat* (head of knowledge) means the mentation of man after undergoing refinement – the transmuted consciousness.[6]

This is not to say that the Templars were Sufis, but it is interesting that the adoration of the Head of the Baphomet is linguistically worthy of connection to the Arabic head of knowledge. Indeed, it was specifically the Crusades that brought the ideas of Islam to Europe, so it is possible that the concept of the *bufihimat* may have been discussed and transmitted, while the Templars fraternized with the Saracens — when not fighting with them.

Another possibility for the origin of the Head relates to the imagery on the first Grand Master's shield, which consisted of three black heads on a gold field.[7] After about two hundred years, it is plausible that this head imagery could have worked itself into the legend of the Baphomet. According to more than one account, the Head was the actual skull of Hugues de Payen, which was preserved as an object of veneration. Then again, a different skull may have received more mystical adoration. "When the Templars were disbanded, a silver head of a woman was found in a preceptory in Paris, and it bore and inscription CAPUT LVIIIM (58M). Henry Lincoln suggests that the M may be implying the symbol for Virgo, the virgin, and he may well be right, for the original virgin was Isis, Goddess of the Templars."[8] Another extremely speculative perspective, that of David Wood, shows "that by applying the Hebrew Atbash code to the name Baphomet, the name Sophia, female wisdom, is revealed. Sophia is equated with Isis by Plutarch."[9]

Admittedly, the unabashedly credulous David Wood can find Isis in a haystack, providing of course that the hay is made of scarab-beetle covered papyrus reeds. His eagerness to factor ancient Egyptian theology into the myth of the Baphomet stretches his credibility, but it leads to some intriguing connections and conclusions regarding Gnosticism and Catharism. That every Templar's personal choice of religion was not strictly Catholic is not surprising. Rather, if the rumors about the Order are to be believed, the head worshipping may have descended from the beliefs and practices of the Gnostic Christians.

Generally, Gnosticism was composed of secretive Christian sects that formed not long after Christ's death. This religion strove to preserve Christ's message as something alive and untainted, but the Gnostics were soon beaten down and damned by the early Catholics as heretical. Gnosticism taught the initiate to seek a direct knowledge of God. He or she "could subscribe to the outward doctrines of any religion, and could continue to operate under many different politico-religious systems."[10] It is noted for its disavowal of materialism and an obsession with dualism. According to the Gnostics, the true God was not the one who created the world — for that was an evil god concerned with base materialism. Instead, God was something outside most people's ability to comprehend, but at the same time, the true God was something that could transcend the evils of the world to give Gnostic understanding to those who were receptive.

Gnostic dualism is present in the figure of the Baphomet, but not exactly in terms of good and evil. Instead we find a spiritual or mystical androgyny, both of sex and ideas. Because of its

## Three Myths

protean ability to be male and female, it draws on and adds to philosophical systems that are sometimes at variance with each other. Over all, the two aspects combine to synthesize a Gestaltic one; one in which the Templars might have found and founded great secrets and mysteries. For the Gnostics, a chief source of divine wisdom was Sophia, a kind of female Christ.

The Cathar *perfecti* wore sacred cords about their waists, which reminds us that the Templars were accused of reverentially touching the Baphomet idol with "small cords, which they wore around themselves next to the shirt or flesh."[11] Indeed, the southwestern region of France, the birthplace of the Order's founder, was a stronghold of not only the Templars, but also the Albigensians, a species of the Cathars. They rejected most of Catholicism's claims regarding the worship of Christ. But, we should be careful in ascribing too much Gnostic influence upon the Templars, because this theory was first published by Friedrich Nicolai, a German Masonic bookseller who promoted the idea that the Templars were sorcerers and Satanists. Whatever the case, the concept of wearing sacred cords was of Gnostic origin. And, speaking of Masonry, it is worthwhile to note that each Masonic Blue Lodge initiation requires the use of a cord, or rather a "cabletow."

For centuries, the ideas of the Templars lay dormant until they were revived in the "higher" degree work of Freemasonry. Around 1736, a Mason named Chevalier Ramsay, "gave Freemasonry a fictional crusading parentage, suggesting that some medieval Crusaders had been both stoneworkers and knightly warriors."[12] With titles like Knight Rose Croix, Knight of the Brazen Serpent, and Knight Kadosh in the Scottish Rite, it is obvious that the legends of Freemasonry made a transition from those of simple stonecutters to those of chivalric crusaders. But was Ramsay's claim precisely fictional? There is evidence that in the early 14th century some Templars escaped to Scotland, thereby achieving diplomatic immunity from the persecutions occurring in France and England. Once in Scotland, some of the Templars were subsumed by the Masonic guilds, which were probably entirely operative in scope at the time. So, it is likely that the Templars influenced the emerging mystical inclinations of Masonry, the legends of which center around the erection of

## Three Myths

the Temple of Solomon — the very edifice that the Templars sought to regain from the Saracens. So, though Ramsay romanticized and perhaps fabricated a Templar heritage to attract a noble audience to the Craft, there still remains the possibility that the Templars indeed infiltrated the early operative lodges.

During the Enlightenment period of European history, the Templars were still regarded as ignominious, so Ramsay did not speak of them specifically when eulogizing the Crusaders. Because the Papal records of the Templar trial remained secret until the Age of Napoleon, actual facts regarding their beliefs were not available and, thus, non-existent. Writers such as Henry Cornelius Agrippa and Guillaume Paradin in the 16th century were capable of turning any wild surmise into a false historical reality and people would believe them. Paradin publicized outrageous rumors about the knighthood, saying that "Templar novices were brought into a 'cave' where they were compelled to worship an image covered with human skin and having two glowing carbuncles for eyes. Here they were made to renounce Christ and to blaspheme and desecrate the cross; then the lights were extinguished in the cave and an orgy took place with the women who had been – inexplicably – admitted."[13] This vilification seems to be synthesized from both the original accusations of head worship and the orgies described in the Byzantine chronicle of Psellus, the crimes of which Agrippa had ascribed to the Templars, as well.

There soon evolved several rival orders of Templars, each claiming secret knowledge and power in a generally Masonic context. While pseudonymous hucksters like Samuel Rosa and George Frederick Johnson exploited initiates by charging consecutively larger fees for each "higher" degree, mystics like Karl Gotthelf von Hund and Johann August Starck sought to legitimize their claims of Templar heritage by digging deeper into Western civilization's past in search of the roots of mysticism. Starck's "Clerks of the Temple" boasted an ancient, eastern source of occult knowledge, which later influenced Count Cagliostro's Egyptian Rite of Freemasonry, which admitted women — a progressiveness that modern Masonry in America sadly lacks. "Starck was apparently the first person to pick out the 'Baphomet' accusation, the charge that the Templars had worshipped a magi-

*Three Myths*

cal image of this name, and to imply clearly both that the charge was true and that the magical properties of the image could be repeated in modern practice. In the ceremony which he designed for the 'consecration' of a 'Canon of the Temple', the altar was occupied by the Bible and an object identified as 'Baphomet',"[14] which was venerated and touched by the initiate who hoped to acquire magical power from the enigmatic entity. If one chooses to believe that the Templar Baphomet was purely the spur-of-the-moment invention of the tortured monks, this incorporation of the Baphomet into Masonic ritual by Starck may be its first true instance of direct worship.

So, the Baphomet took centuries to re-emerge from the moldy rumors of the Templars' fall. When it did, the people who spoke of it took great liberties in explaining the meaning of the mythological beast.

## THE BAPHOMET IN THE 19th CENTURY

Considering that Starck's Clerks of the Temple and von Hund's Strict Templar Observance were Masonic orders that were merely suffused with medieval flavoring, Templarism seemed to have lost its direct lineage, at least until the early 19th century. In 1804, a French physician and Freemason named Bernard Raymond Fabré-Palaprat claimed to have discovered "some documents proving the existence of an uninterrupted succession of Templar 'Grand Masters,' operating secretly from the suppression of the order in 1307 to 1792 (when the last 'hidden' Grand Master, Duke Louis Hercule Timoléon de Crossé-Brissac, died in Versailles, massacred by the Jacobins)."[15] His partner (a man named Ledru who happened to be Crossé-Brissac's doctor) forged a document known as the 'Larmenius Charter,' which contained the signatures of each spurious post-1312 Templar Grand Master, which included De Molay's supposed successor and less-likely historical figures. In 1805, Fabré-Palaprat proclaimed himself the new Grand Master of the Templar Order, which sought to make itself distinct from Freemasonry. On the 500th anniversary of De Molay's arrest, Fabré-Palaprat held a ceremony in honor of the martyred knight. So, though the Larmenius Charter promoted an illegitimate legacy, it succeeded in restoring at least the myths of the Templars.

## Three Myths

The Baphomet was most radically re-interpreted by Alphonse Louis Constant, a French occultist who called himself Eliphas Levi. Originally a priest, he was reprimanded for preaching non-Catholic doctrine. Thus defrocked, he married a 16-year-old woman who bore him two children before seeking and obtaining matrimonial annulment. Levi then settled down to write pamphlets about socialism and books about ceremonial magic. Strangely, he was inspired by a mystic transvestite named Ganneau. The 19th century was rife with eccentric occultists and indeed, Levi should be classified as one.

Levi maintained a paradoxical viewpoint about black magic, his favorite topic. While credulously expounding knowledge about conjuration, he protected himself with the following syllogistic proof against the existence of an actual Satan:

> As a superior personality and power, Satan does not exist. He is the personification of all errors, perversities, and consequently of all weakness. If God may be defined as He Who exists of necessity, may we not define His antagonist and enemy as he who does not exist at all? The absolute affirmation of good implies an absolute negation of evil: so also in the light, the shadow is luminous.[16]

Colin Wilson denounces Levi by calling him a charlatan, albeit an unconscious one. Admittedly, the man's descriptions of the practice of magic were hyperbolic and he tended to fabricate unsubstantiated details everywhere in his writing. But what of the Baphomet? Levi's shoddy cabalistic rearranging of the word yielded, "Tem Oph Ab," which was the abbreviation of some mistranslated Latin. But for all his faults, Levi became an influential writer on occult subjects. Indeed, he solidified the myth and imagery of the Baphomet.

Levi's picture of the Baphomet is a "synthesis of deformities" which shows a cross-legged, hermaphroditic, goat-god with angel wings and horns. The figure rests its feet upon a globe, as it sits on a cube, which (like the Masonic finished ashlar) suggests perfection. Denoting generativity, a tantric caduceus (like the one belonging to Hermes) rises above a scaly belly. Two arms

*Three Myths*

Eliphas Levi's Baphomet

## Three Myths

point up and down, which are labeled "Solve" and "Coagula," respectively. One interpretation of this gesture suggests the unity of the polarities of the dissolving qualities of water and the coagulating attributes of fire, as mentioned in many alchemical texts. Being hermaphroditic in character, Baphomet is imbued with the power of reconciling opposites. Levi intends the two crescent moons to represent the balance between white and black magic. They also represent the cabalistic spheres of *Geburah* and *Chesed*, which mean severity and mercy, respectively.

The diabolical idol had been a vague, variegated rumor before Levi's creation of the Baphomet as a glyph, a symbolic representation rife with pagan meaning. Perhaps he was inspired by the masonry of a cathedral, specifically the horned gargoyles. While exclaiming that the Templars definitely worshipped the idol, he explains that the Baphomet was not the figure of the Devil, but rather the god Pan, "the god of our modern schools of philosophy, the god of the Alexandrian theurgic school, and of our own mystical Neo-platonists ... the god of the primitive Gnostic schools; the Christ also of the dissident priesthood."[17] This last qualification he ascribes to the goat of Black Magic, the Goat of Mendes. He goes on to explain the pentagram on the beast's forehead, which he says is representative of humanity's partial control over the four elements: earth, air, fire, and water. The pentacle is the sign of the Microcosm, as opposed to the Seal of Solomon, the six-sided pictograph of the Macrocosm. Levi believed that one could conjure and contain spirits by means of a pentagram, a belief which belies concepts set forth elsewhere in his book. The Goat of Mendes "bears upon its forehead the Sign of the Pentagram with one point in the ascendant, which is sufficient to distinguish it as a symbol of light."[18]

Indeed, the torch of knowledge burns upon its crowned, centered horn. Thus, the Baphomet becomes a Promethean figure.

*Three Myths*

As the Greco-Roman god who first gave humans fire, Prometheus is also understood by many to be a mythic expression of Lucifer. The Satanic attributes of a defiant god relate in the Judaic legend to the tempter in the Garden of Eden. And, as Breck Outland explains in an accompanying essay about the myth of the Phoenix, fire symbolizes sexual embrace at the moment of orgasm. Most forms of Paganism agree upon the worship of Nature and their mysteries bespeak the magic of reproduction. So, the Baphomet is not actually evil, but it remains too bestial for canonization in any faith aside from Satanism.

After making an allusion to the figure of Lucifer, Levi finally admits that "the dread Baphomet henceforth, like all monstrous idols, enigmas of antique science and its dreams, is only an innocent and even pious hieroglyph."[19] Even though Levi was convinced of the veracity of his re-invented Baphomet, we must be skeptical, remaining suspicious of his constant prevarication regarding occult matters. Even the flamboyant A. E. Waite thought of Levi as a writer who was too imaginative, subjective, and naïve. But, his skewed (or uneven) knowledge of Cabalism and the Tarot notwithstanding, Levi made a great impression upon Aleister Crowley, a man who declared himself the Great Beast 666. But, that is not the extent of Crowley's adulation of Levi. The Englishman actually proclaimed himself to be the reincarnation of the Frenchman.

# THE BAPHOMET IN THE 20th CENTURY

As he was a master of occult sciences, no magus in this century has surpassed the occasionally evil Aleister Crowley. His strict upbringing in a puritanical Christian family caused him to reject the messianic tradition in favor of Eastern religious practices like *yoga* and *tantra*. During his life, he traveled through exotic countries (including Egypt and Tibet) searching for the sources of ancient hidden wisdom. After leaving the Hermetic Order of the Golden Dawn around the turn of the century, Crowley eventually formed his own mystical order, The Argenteum Astrum (A.'.A.'.), or Silver Star. In 1904, he claimed to have contacted an extraterrestrial intelligence who revealed itself as Aiwass, Crowley's Holy Guardian Angel. The resultant trance-written

## Three Myths

*Book of the Law* is a cryptic combination of Egyptian mythology, spiritualistic Theosophy, and Qabalism, as it was spelled by him. Shown here is a photograph of the first commercial edition of *The Book of the Law* has Crowley's "Baphomet" signature. He used this name as his official, exoteric title in the Ordo Templi Orientis (OTO), a Masonic Templar order that originated in Germany. The founder of this Order, Karl Kellner, was the first person to assume the forbidden name, but Crowley was the one who tried to live up to its blasphemous reputation. Since he was an obstreperous Golden Dawn heresiarch, it is no surprise that he published their secret rituals in the *Equinox* after securing control of the British branch of the OTO.

Like Levi, Crowley saw the figure of Baphomet as the Master of Creation. To this concept Crowley also brought an aspect of sexual magick [sic] to the forefront. For him, this goat-headed, hermaphroditic god was a symbolic union of the four elements and the conjoined sexes distilled into a fifth element of creative spirit. As in Levi, this quintessence is represented by the upright pentagram of human intelligence emblazoned on Baphomet's brow beneath the flaming torch of divine revelation that is fixed between its bestial horns. Crowley explicitly linked the Baphomet with Sirius, or Sothis, a binary star that has been associated with the Egyptian god Set. Michael Aquino, the Ipsissmus of the

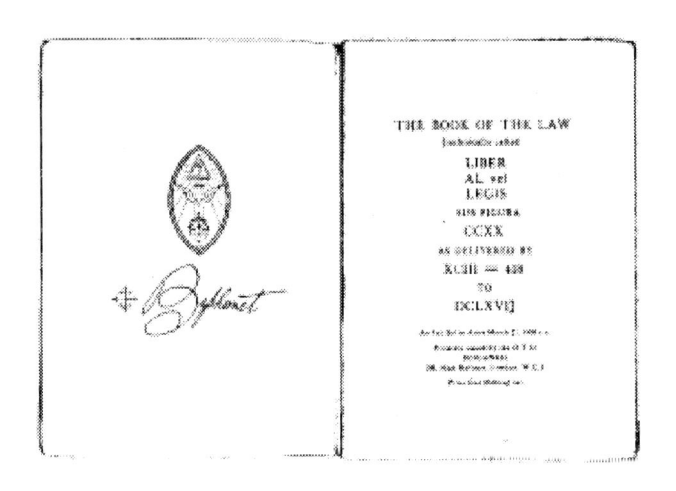

Crowley's Baphomet signature

*Three Myths*

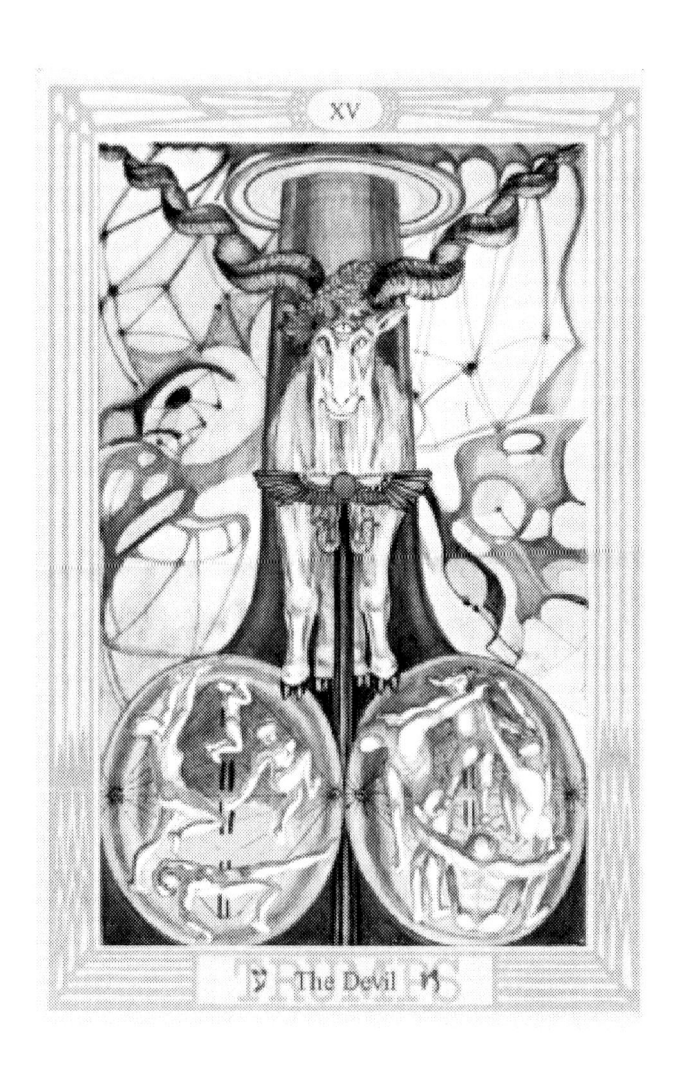

Baphomet as depicted in the Tarot
(Copyright © 1978 by U.S. Games, Inc.)

## Three Myths

Temple of Set, describes the god as a Satanic archetype. Not surprisingly, the newspapers decried Crowley as a Satanist, though he was actually more of a Gnostic pagan.

He believed himself to be a personification of the Baphomet, as he wrote:

> Now shalt thou adore me who am the Eye and the Tooth, the Goat of the Spirit, the Lord of Creation. I am the Eye in the Triangle, the Silver Star that ye adore. I am Baphomet, that is the Eightfold Word that shall be equilibrated with the Three. There is no act or passion that shall not be a hymn in mine honour.[20]

Though opaque and obfuscating on the surface, the references to the Eye and the Tooth are easily explained. The Eye, or *Ayin* as it is called in Hebrew, corresponds to the constellation *Capricornus* and also the Tarot trump, the Devil. Note the uncannily prophetic conjunction of the doubly helical goat horns with the syzygy of the fertilized eggs. These peopled ova also form the testicles of a phallus, in front of which is depicted a three-eyed goat. Astrological images of *Capricornus* show it as having the head and torso of a goat and the scaly tail of a fish. The goat in this instance also signifies the lusty woodland god Pan, the pagan deity investigated earlier. The Tooth, or *Shin* as it is known in Qabalism, represents the element of Fire and also the Spirit of Primal Life Force. This fire of life is depicted in Crowley's Devil/Baphomet by a Horus-winged variant of the caduceus of Hermes. This symbol embodies the qualities of both healing and the powerful energies of Kundalini (an element of sex magick), as represented by the serpents entwined around the winged wand, which springs from its genitals. In fact, "*Shin*" together with the letter "*Tet*," which means snake, forms the glyph for Shaitan, or Satan. It also translates as the "Fire Snake," which is possibly the same icon used by tantric adepts to describe how sexual energy flows within the body. Perhaps this explains how the mythic Satan (or the Devil) was transformed from his early image as a snake in the Garden of Eden to his later incarnation as the goat-god Baphomet.

## Three Myths

Crowley's most significant contribution to religious freedom is summed up in his dictum, "Do what thou wilt shall be the whole of the Law, Love is the Law, Love under Will," a philosophical amalgamation of Rabelais and Nietzsche. A superficial reading of this statement suggests that the Thelemite, the name for a practitioner of Crowley's strong-willed philosophy, can excuse any action, no matter the moral consequences. The ultimate expression of this naïve understanding of the Law of Thelema is The Church of Satan, which will be discussed momentarily. But, for now, we must clearly state that Crowley intended no such simplification. Rather, when he wrote that "every man and every woman is a star,"[21] he believed that each person has a unique calling in life, the goal of which is achieved by means of applying the sacred will, a purpose tempered by love. Indeed, the Great Beast 666 was a selfish man with unconventional morals, but he was not, in fact, a Satanist. So, although he performed infernal rituals that scandalized him and his followers, Crowley was instead a champion of the human spirit. And, as Thelemites believe, he initiated the Age of Horus, "the Aeon of the 'Crowned and Conquering Child' [that will] see the blending of the two sexes [that denote the Ages of Isis and Osiris] as one. The bisexual Baphomet of the Templars symbolizes this concept."[22]

When Crowley died in 1947, his disciples founded many fractionalized branches of the OTO. Typically, each one claimed to be the true magickal heir. The most successful of these bickering groups set up camp in California, where Hollywood stars found it thrilling to toy with occultism. There, the "Do What Thou Wilt" philosophy was picked up and exploited by a circus lion-tamer and organist named Anton Szandor LaVey. His definition of Satanic magic, "the change in situations or events in accordance with one's will, which would, using normally accepted methods, be unchangeable,"[23] is nearly identical to Crowley's (non-Satanic) definition of magick, the Will's ability to supernaturally affect the phenomenal world

Church of Satan logo

## Three Myths

without interfering with others' Wills. In 1966, LaVey announced the formation of the Church of Satan and adopted the Baphomet, pentagonal and stylized, as the religion's central icon. At the five points of the encircled star there are placed Hebrew letters, which supposedly spell out the word "Leviathan."[24]

By insisting that "Satanism demands study – not worship,"[25] LaVey's atheistic rituals ring hollowly. His incorporation of Enochian conjuration seems out of place in a religion that prides itself on its atheistic bias. Crowley believed in the magick he preached, but LaVey winks slyly when invoking Satan or lesser demons. His nine Satanic statements promote a fusion of social Darwinism and anti-Christian indulgence. Peter Gilmore, a devotee, defines contemporary Satanism as "a brutal religion of elitism and social Darwinism that seeks to re-establish the reign of the able over the idiotic, of swift justice over injustice, and for a wholesale rejection of egalitarianism as a myth that has crippled the advancement of the human species for the last two thousand years."[26]

And, indeed, some of LaVey's statements resound with truth, especially when, through application, they expose the paradoxical selfishness of altruism. Laid out similarly to the *Book of the Law*, the *Satanic Bible* asks, "are we not all predatory animals by instinct? If humans ceased wholly from preying upon each other, could they continue to exist?"[27] LaVey urges people to live for the moment and to gratify their willful desires. Foremost, he promotes the idea that each self-aware person is actually a god, a concept that is also popular with lucrative New Age faiths. Popularity, wealth, and fame were exactly Anton's goals and, through application of his will, he received all three. Though in its early years The Church of Satan drew membership from the likes of Sammy Davis, Jr. and Jayne Mansfield, today its membership mostly consists of angry teenaged adherents who are merely reacting to Christianity, which makes this Satanic organization a sub-set of the sprawling Judeo-Christian myth. The Church of Satan is rigidly hierarchical and, like Scientology, advancement through the ranks can cost a considerable amount of money.

## Three Myths

Mocking the right-hand path's outrageous claims of the goings-on of the Black Mass, the Black Pope evokes imagery of the Baphomet and the crimes attributed to the Templars:

> If the Devil appears he is invariably in the form of a rather eager man wearing the head of a black goat upon his shoulders. Then follows a potpourri of flagellation, prayer-book burning, fellatio, and general hindquarters kissing – all done to a background of ribald recitations from the Holy Bible, and audible expectorations on the cross! If a baby can be slaughtered during the ritual, so much the better; for as everyone knows, this is the favorite sport of the Satanist.[28]

It should be mentioned at this point that the Church of Satan does not promote child sacrifice; not because of fears of sin, but rather because the ritualistic murder of the innocent is seen as pointless. But, as Richard Ramirez (the Night Stalker) attests, murder is permissible for the Satanist, though it will continue to be punished as a serious crime by society. At his arraignment, Ramirez flashed LaVey's sign of the Baphomet, an encircled pentagram, that he had carved or drawn upon his palm.

Approximately contemporaneous with the founding of the Church of Satan, The Process Church of the Final Judgement was a flamboyant millenarian cult that has been repeatedly accused of Satanic crime, though no evidence supports such claims. True, the cult worshipped Satan and Lucifer as deific principles, but members were also taught to revere Christ and Jehovah in order to balance dark with light. The goal of the movement was to force these left- and right-hand paths of mysticism to converge. Robert and Maryanne DeGrimston, the founders of the Process, foresaw this union as occurring during the End Times and they wanted to spread a warning to all. Around 1974, the cult disbanded amid vague rumors of child sacrifice and ritual murder, but in reality the divorce of the founders was the true cause of dissolution. No Process member on (available) record ever committed a serious crime. Indeed, greater crimes of libel were committed against the Process, especially by Ed Sanders

## Three Myths

and Maury Terry, voices of pernicious misinformation amid an already confused Mass Media.

Originally, the DeGrimstons followed and taught Scientology, a non-diabolical science fiction self-help religion with Thelemic roots. While roaming North America and Europe, primarily, the Process spread the message that, in the End Times, the forces and good and evil would be reconciled. Their central tautological precept propounded that:

> Christ said: Love thine enemy. Christ's enemy was Satan and Satan's enemy was Christ. Through love, enmity is destroyed. Through love, saint and sinner destroy the enmity between them. Through love, Christ and Satan have destroyed Their enmity and come together for the End; Christ to judge and Satan to execute the judgement.[29]

This self-consistent, though skewed, logic disallowed external questioning of the philosophy. DeGrimston continued with the following rhetoric:

> Salvation is the resolution of conflict. The ultimate salvation is the salvation of God. The ultimate conflict is God and Anti-God. God and Anti-God are two halves of a divided totality. And they ultimately must be reconciled. God and Anti-God are embodied in Christ and Satan. So Christ and Satan must be reconciled. The Lamb and the Goat must come together. Pure love descended from the pinnacle of heaven, united with pure hatred raised from the depths of Hell.[30]

Of course, the "Goat" he refers to hails from Mendes. The Process ceremonies provided a balance between light and dark, good and evil. Representations of the Gods were arranged dynamically opposite from each other. The Baphomet faced a white cross and a basin of water was countered by a bowl of flame, the only significant source of light present during the Sabbath. The Sacrifist and the Evangelist presided over the ceremonies, vouching for Christ and Satan, respectively. Both the cross and the goat-head adorned the infamous Process black robes that were worn with exceeding bravado by the members as they preached their End Times philosophy, in public as well as in their gothic, private cloisters.

Called the Badge of Mendes, the humanoid Baphomet here indicated the Processean's acceptance of the power of Satan. The badge consisted of a "black triangle, pointed downward, bearing the head of Levi's goat in red. The face is half-man, half-goat. Between the two spreading horns is a crown, while the forehead is imprinted with a magical pentagram. The Cross and the Goat always went together but were always kept physically separate – for example, at opposite ends of the Alpha ritual room or at separate points on [their] uniforms."[31]

Process baphomet

What follows is an example of The Process' presentation of their own variable mythology, which explains their interpretation of the difference between Satan and Lucifer. The below text was a response to a letter that asked about the Process figure of Lucifer. The sixth issue of the *Process* magazine answered at length:

> Recently, we came upon the following quotations from the *Dictionary of Angels* by Gustav Davidson, which coincides with our own knowledge of Lucifer.
>
> "LUCIFER: ("light giver") – erroneously equated with the (supposedly) fallen angel (Satan) due to a misreading of Isaiah 14:12: 'How art thou fallen from heaven, O Lucifer, son of the morning,' an apostrophe which applied to Nebuchadnezzar, king of Babylon (but see under Satan). It should be pointed out that the authors of the books of the Old Testament knew nothing of fallen or evil angels, and do

## Three Myths

not mention them, although at times as in Job 4:18, the Lord 'put no trust' in his angels and 'charged them with Folly', which would indicate that angels were not all they should be. The name Lucifer was applied to Satan by St. Jerome and other Christian Fathers."

We can go some way towards explaining how this misconception came to be given credence.

Christ is the Spirit of Unity. But the early Church, chiefly under the direction of St. Paul who had been a devout Pharisee before his conversion on the road to Damascus, gave Christianity a heavy Jehovian bias, to which it has clung ever since. Therefore it is understandable that Lucifer would become identified with the 'Adversary,' which is Satan.

Now it is true that Lucifer's Light, which includes all of life's gentler pleasures and indulgences, CAN lead a human being into the realms of greed, excess, dependence, materialism, and demand for more and more and more. And that is indeed Satan's territory. But it is equally true that Jehovah's rigid puritanism CAN lead a human being into the realms of bigotry, intolerance, cruelty, repression, prejudice, and war. That is what happened to Christianity – the Crusades, the Inquisition, witch hunting, and other highlights of the Church's history are the stark illustrations of this trend. And that too is Satan's territory.

Jehovah rules the Christian Church, so Lucifer is identified with the Devil. But Satan takes his toll of the fallen, Jehovian and Luciferian alike. And finally, here is what the *Dictionary of Angels* says of Satan Himself.

"SATAN: the Hebrew meaning of the word is 'adversary'. In Numbers 22:22 that angels of the Lord stands against Balaam 'for an adversary' (satan). In other Old Testament Books (Job, Chronicles, Psalms,

*Three Myths*

> Zachariah) the term likewise designates an office: and the angel investing that office is not apostate or fallen. He becomes such in early New Testament times and writings, when he emerges as Satan (capitol 'S'), the prince of evil and enemy of GOD…"
>
> Another concept which coincides with our own knowledge. Satan fulfills a function on behalf of GOD – not an enviable function, but a necessary one if the human game is to run its course. And as long as human beings BLAME Satan for the evil in themselves, instead of acknowledging His real purpose which is to bring out that evil and expose it, there can be no redemption.[32]

The Process theology reminds us of Jungian alchemical archetypes, but it also reflects the psychological states of the founders. Essentially a cult of personalities, The Process faded out before 1975. But, in their hey-day, they took seriously their pledge to explore evil with equal doses of good.

Today, The Process falsely continues as a pet-cult for industrial rock bands. Genesis P-Orridge (née Neil Megson), a Thelemite with a severe spelling problem, was originally involved with two prominent experimental rock bands, Throbbing Gristle and Psychic TV. In 1981 he founded Thee Temple ov Psychick Youth [sic] and, with it, he planned to hypnotize people via his artsy-evil music videos while zapping them with fiendish emeters, the psycho-technological tool of the Scientologists. Realizing that he was no longer young, he dropped TOPY in the early 1990's and now proclaims himself a top Processean, but without DeGrimston's sanction. No other claims of legitimacy are available to P-Orridge, though, since he has left behind most of the Process theology. Rather, he is content merely exploiting the group's mythology and symbolism. Recently, he was exiled from England due to unfounded rumors of his participation in baby sacrifice.

*Three Myths*

Original Process logo   Genesis P-Orridge's "Process" logo

Truly, the only still-touring rock band with a legitimate connection to the original Process is George Clinton's P-Funk All Stars. During the earliest years of the 1970's, George Clinton's heavily LSD-influenced psyche was attracted to visions of apocalypse. In this capacity, he was impressed by The Process enough to prompt him to include DeGrimston's writing on Fear and America as liner notes in the *Maggot Brain* and *America Eats Its Young* albums, respectively. Both rants appear in the CD re-releases of these popular, ground-breaking and booty-shaking funk albums and, as such, the excerpts remain the most widely dispersed examples of DeGrimston's writing today, even though Clinton has nothing but memories about the Process now. Just as P-Orridge was never a proper member of the cult, neither was Clinton. But, the Baphomet lives on at his concerts by means of a hand gesture collectively given by his audience. in a P-Funk cartoon, the index and pinky fingers extend in adoration of the Baphomet. Whether or not the *genuflecteur* is aware of it, each person giving the sign actually invokes the pagan goat-god in all its frenzied glory.

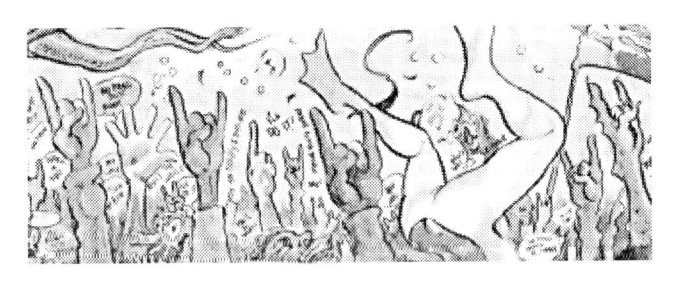

P-Funk fans flash the sign of the Baphomet

## CONCLUSION

While speaking in Dallas, Texas in 1995, Robert Anton Wilson, a scholar of conspiracy theory, concluded that a small cult within the ranks of the Templars indeed worshipped a head called Baphomet, but that eager Inquisitors ascribed and perpetuated much more significance to the adoration than was appropriate. "Many Templars confessed to having seen this idol, but as they described it differently, we must suppose that it was not in all cases represented under the same form."[33] So, in all likelihood, the Baphomet would never have received the public veneration that it now enjoys (within the Church of Satan, for instance), had not the Inquisitors forced its exposure. As we have seen, the Protean creature has assumed many roles and purposes since its inception into the annals of occultism.

Explained dispassionately, the Baphomet is merely a resonant myth that should not be interpreted as evil. Instead, it is a glyph that describes the reconciliation of opposites: male and female, bestial and godly, light and dark. But, through ignorance, this pagan symbol will probably continue to be maligned far into the next millenium, since few people are willing to consider that a good goat-god could possibly exist. Since the time of Christianity's victory over the Greco-Roman religions, the horned goat has been a symbol of a rapacious appetite. No one seems to understand the goat's true purpose, which is simply to exist as one of Nature's beautiful creatures. Nothing on this planet can truly be evil, except for humans, for it is we who have defined evil. And, in doing so, it is we who have lived up to the expectations of the definition.

## ACKNOWLEDGEMENTS

Foremost, I should thank my grandmother, Margaret Jackson, for her loving tolerance of my interest in the occult. Also, I am grateful for the editing assistance rendered by three exceedingly lovely red-heads: Julie Keene, Julie Morrow, and Lori Eaton. And, finally, thanks to Rodney Perkins and Phillip Walker for persisting in accomplishing the lay-out for this book.

## ENDNOTES

[1] Burman, Edward. *The Templars: Knights of God*. Rochester, VT: Destiny Books, 1986. p. 80.
[2] Daraul, Arkon [pseudonym of Idries Shah]. *A History of Secret Societies*. Secaucus, NJ: Citadel Press, 1961. p. 56.
[3] Michelet, M. *Proces de Templiers*. Paris, 1851. p. 383.
[4] Howard, Michael. *The Occult Conspiracy*. Rochester, VT: Destiny Books, 1989. p. 37.
[5] Daraul. p. 42.
[6] Shah, Idries. *The Sufis*. New York: Anchor Books, 1971. p. 254.
[7] Baigent, Michael, Richard Leigh, Henry Lincoln *Holy Blood, Holy Grail*. New York: Dell, 1983. p. 82.
[8] Wood, David. *Genisis*. Tunbridge Wells, Kent: Baton Press, 1985. p. 123.
[9] Schonfield, Hugh. *The Essene Odyssy*. Element Books, 1984. p.164.
[10] Daurul, p. 84.
[11] Barber, Malcolm. *The Trial of the Templars*. Cambridge: Cambridge University Press, 1978. p. 249.
[12] Partner, *The Murdered Magicians*. New York: Barnes & Noble Books, 1987. p.103.
[13] Partner, p. 94.
[14] Partner, p. 121.
[15] Introvigne, Massimo. "Ordeal by Fire: The Tragedy of the Solar Temple." in *Religion* Vol. 25 #3. London: Academic Press, 1995. p. 268.
[16] Levi, Eliphas. *Transcendental Magic: Its Doctrine and Ritual*. Translated by A. E. Waite. London: Braken Books, 1995. p. 379.
[17] Levi, p. 376.
[18] Ibid., p. 377.
[19] Ibid., p. 378.
[20] Crowley, Aleister. *Liber A'ash, vel Capricorni Pneumatici*. In *Portable Darkness* edited by Scott Michaelsen. New York: Harmony Books, 1989. p. 171.
[21] Crowley, Aiwass, and Ra-Hoor-Khuit. *The Book of the Law*. Manuscript 1904. p.1.

[22] Grant, Kennth. *Aleister Crowley and the Hidden God.* New York: Samuel Weiser, 1974. pp. 65-66.

[23] LaVey, Anton Szandor. *The Satanic Bible*. New York: Avon Books, 1969. p. 110.

[24] Barton, Blanche. The Secret Life of a Satanist. Los Angeles: Feral House, 1990. p. 84.

[25] LaVey. *The Satanic Rituals*. New York: Avon Books, 1972. p. 19.

[26] Gilmore, Peter H. "Satanism: the Feared Religion" from *http://webpages.marshall.edu/~allen12/feared.txt*, quoted on July 11, 1997.

[27] LaVey. *The Satanic Bible*. p. 33.

[28] Ibid., p. 99.

[29] *Process on Fear*. Number 5, 1970. p. 20.

[30] Ibid., p. 21.

[31] Bainbridge, William Sims. Satan's Power. Berkeley: University of California Press, 1978. p. 186.

[32] *Process on Death*. Number 6, 1971. p. 14

[33] *Narratives of Sorcery and Magic*. Quoted from *An Encyclopedia of Occultism* by Lewis Spence. New York: Citadel Press, 1993. p. 63.

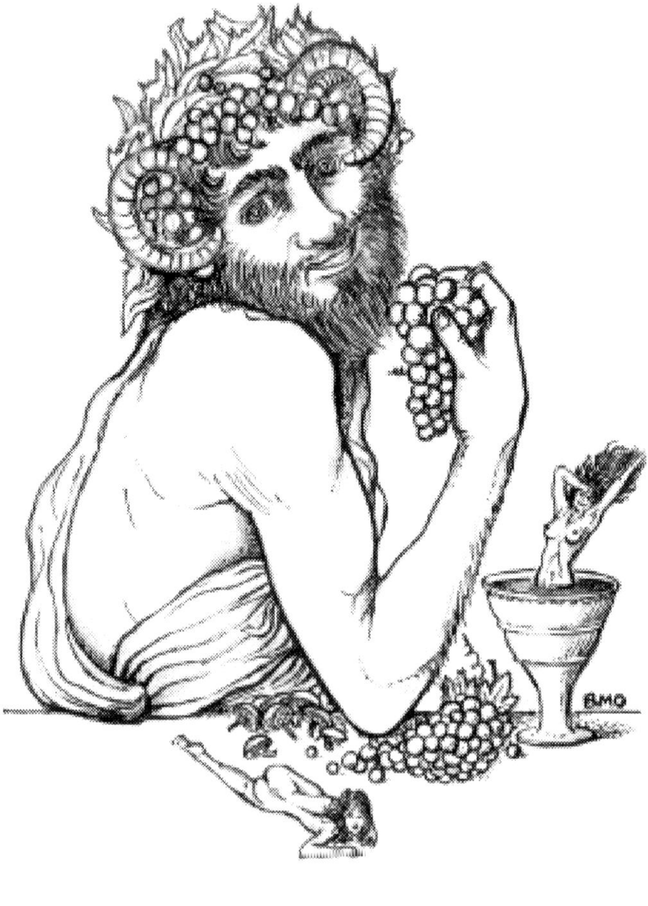

# The Mad God's Sacraments
# by Steve Aydt

In 1936, a secret society of artists and writers, calling themselves the Acéphale Society, gathered in the woods near Saint-Nom for the first time. One of the eleven primary goals of the "headless" society was the participation "in the destruction of the world as it presently exists, with eyes wide open to the world which is yet to be,"[1] an objective worthy of the most lurid pulp fiction of the period.

Shrouded in disinformation, paradox, and mystery, Acéphale was described by seminal member Georges Bataille as "ferociously religious."[2] But Acéphale was ferociously religious even as it dispensed with God, invoking a Nietzschean vision of a Dionysian superhuman. Celebrant Andre Masson sketched the ironic and victorious figure of the headless emblem of Acéphale — "our Master Dionysus," its sex masked by the skull of its own severed head. Arms stretched wide, it clutches a sharp dagger in its left hand and a blazing heart in its right. Stars cover its nipples while the digestive tract is a labyrinth. Masson clarified that the burning heart was that of Dionysus and not "the Crucified," as Acéphale was fervently anti-Christian. In *The Sacred Conspiracy*, Bataille describes the vision:

> Beyond what I am, I meet a being who makes me laugh because he is headless; he fills me with dread because he is made of innocence and crime; he holds a steel weapon in his left hand, flames like those of a sacred heart in his right. He is not a man. He is not

a God either. He is not me but he is more than me: his stomach is the labyrinth in which he has lost himself, loses me with him, and in which I discover myself as him, in other words as a monster.[3]

Members of Acéphale aspired to a collective experience, one in which individual desires would be unified and collectively consecrated. Inner vision would be utilized as a seed, something which would germinate and sprout into manifestation, an ivy which would thrive and transform the world. "Mystery had two faces, one turned outside and the other inside, the inside being tumult and chaos, and the outside the surpassing with a view to a new order."[4]

Bataille declared, "It is time to abandon the world of the civilized and its light."[5] His vision of a genuinely conspiratorial secret society included rites of initiation, rituals, and a separation of adepts from the profane world. Since nothing would reveal this to the external world, members considered themselves as part of an invisible realm, one coexisting with the mundane consensus. Regarding the rituals of Acéphale, initiates told stories of a voyage out of the world. Nietzsche, a prominent influence on the society, wrote of the change wrought by such an experience:

> What is strangest is this: afterward one has a different taste — a second taste. Out of such abysses, also out of the abyss of great suspicion, one returns newborn, having shed one's skin, more ticklish and sarcastic, with a more delicate taste for joy, with a more tender tongue for all good things, with gayer senses, with a second dangerous innocence in joy, more childlike and yet a hundred times more subtle than one has ever been before."[6]

Over time, the rites of Dionysus have taken place in a shadow realm — a place outside of accepted history and far from the religions of the cities. Those who have visited this realm and returned are not the same as they were before. Dionysus, naturally enough, wore a wide variety of masks in different times

## Three Myths

and cultures. This ancient faith came to Greece from Phrygia and Asia Minor. It was the hallmark of thousands of years of Minoan spirituality, each successive King Minos presiding over the sect of the bull-headed deity originally known as Zan. This god has known many names since that time, including Zagreus, Shiva, Bacchus, Cernunnos and even Robin Goodfellow, the unruly god of the forest depicted in the Robin Hood legends. In whatever guise the wild god appears, he presides over madcap pranks, harmony with Nature, initiatory rites, and ecstatic bliss. As Shiva, he is the Lord of Yoga. Wherever he is worshipped, he is identified with the erect phallus and is even considered its divine embodiment.

It seems probable that this faith was rooted in ancient shamanism. In seeing Dionysus torn to shreds and devoured by the Titans, we witness the echo of the shaman's experience of being ripped apart in the underworld by spirits who devour his flesh. But, when he is reconstituted, the shaman is in possession of power derived from the spirits who ate of his flesh, just as celebrants who have eaten the sacramental flesh of Dionysus merge with the god in spirit.

Dionysus was an outsider, an alien god whose rites earned him a place of honor in many pantheons. Yet over two millennia, Dionysian spirituality has been almost systematically eradicated in the Western world. The temples of the Mystery Religions were sacked and destroyed. And tight cultural and legal restrictions continue to weigh heavily upon Dionysian sacraments to this day, as we shall see.

Intimations of the drunken god have traveled across time and space on thought waves, illustrations on pottery, folk songs, and fairy tales, toward a dimly glimpsed horizon. These self-perpetuating bits of information have traveled from person to person, like a flu of the mind or a spiritual virus. Over time, the sacraments of Dionysus have changed with the god, so the savagery of rent flesh is a dim and distant memory. But the sacraments of the god have always been controversial, as have their effects.

Artists have continued to transmit the voice of the Mystery as they have best been able to convey it. This voice, as in the Pentecostal gift, speaks in a secret tongue which may be interpreted by those who are prepared to listen closely. The tongue of Dionysus is the strange language of Nature. So, in order to more clearly understand what is being communicated, we should first examine the myths, mysteries, and many faces of the god. Secondly, we will survey the sacraments and techniques employed in Dionysian initiations and secret societies. And we shall examine the factors which drove one of the world's oldest religions underground. But it is in the nature of the born-again god to sprout from the underworld, as we shall see when we examine some of the more contemporary manifestations of Dionysus in the arts and in the creative realms beyond art and philosophy.

Mystery Religions operate on the mind and spirit through the sensorium, so we will conclude by examining the impact of mass media on human consciousness. What is the role of Dionysian spirituality in a world largely girdled by an ever expanding electronic virtual reality which operates by dominating the primary senses of sight and hearing? Can the paradisiacal visions of animistic religions be sustained in the face of cancerous technological expansion and development?

## THE NATIVITY AND MASKS OF DIONYSUS

Like Jesus, who followed him in time and pattern, Dionysus was the result of the union between a mortal woman and a god. Semele, the daughter of Cadmus, the King and founder of Thebes, was seduced by the god Zeus and impregnated. Zeus's jealous wife, Hera, devised the undoing of his consort, suggesting to her that if Zeus truly loved her he would reveal himself to her in all his divine glory. When Semele asked this favor of Zeus, she

## Three Myths

reminded him that he had promised to honor her every wish. With regret, Zeus revealed himself in his true form as the lightning god, blasting Semele with blazing intensity. But the same sacred fire that destroyed Semele rendered their unborn son immortal. Zeus was able to snatch him from her womb even as Semele disintegrated, sewing the fetus into his thigh where it would complete its gestation period. When the child came to full term, the birth was assisted by Hermes, the Greek god of magic and writing, who swaddled the newborn in a golden cloth. For a while, Dionysus was raised by Semele's sister, Ino. But, the vengeful Hera enchanted Ino, causing her to hurl herself into the sea with one of her two sons. Zeus later transformed Ino into a deity of the seas — Leucothea, the White Goddess. Meanwhile, Hermes transformed Dionysus into a ram to fool the wrathful Hera and spirited away the child-god to Mount Nysa, where he was nurtured by the nymphs Macris, Nysa, Erato, Bacche, and Bromie on milk and honey. While there, he pioneered the art of wine-making.

In the Orphic legend of the death of the child Dionysus at the hands of the Titans and his subsequent rebirth, we find a pattern used by the ancient Mystery Religion of Orphism. In this account, Zeus appeared to his daughter Persephone as a serpent, seducing and impregnating her. While in the Underworld, she gave birth to Dionysus Zagreus, a bull-horned infant wreathed in serpents and destined by Zeus to be the ruler of the world. But the Titans — the Great Old Ones of mythology — were incensed. Filled with jealousy and hatred, they distracted the infant god with a mirror and then tore him to pieces (the ritual reenactment of which was known as *sparagmos*). They then proceeded to cook and devour every part of him except his heart, which was stolen by Athene and returned to Zeus. Prior to blasting the Titans to ashes, Zeus gobbled the baby's heart and later ejaculated its divine essence into Semele, impregnating her with Dionysus, as previously mentioned.

## Three Myths

The combination of these two nativity tales accounts for one of the titles of Dionysus — "thrice born." From the ashes of the Titans, humanity supposedly emerged. This root of Orphic duality sprouted from the idea that the human body was made of base and evil matter (Titan's ashes), a tomb to be escaped through refinement of spirit (the essence of Dionysus contained in those ashes).

Georges Bataille's intention to abandon the light of civilization demonstrates a rejection of this Orphic depiction of Dionysus, perhaps as a domestication of the deity. In Orphism, the dark chthonic energy of Dionysus, symbolized by the serpent, is balanced against the Apollonian light of reason. And it is this light that Bataille rejects in his paradoxically atheistic theology: "The *acéphalic man* mythologically expresses sovereignty committed to destruction and the death of God, and in this the identification with the headless man merges and melds with the identification of the superhuman, which is entirely 'the death of God.'"[7] Bataille's view of the idea of God as a prison, or at least a restriction, parodies the tunnel-vision of theologians. Here are the boundaries of orthodoxy — that religion functions as an oppressive force that is more concerned with social control than with spirituality.

What the Orphic and the Eleusinian Mystery Religions did accomplish was a shift from religions of the state to a spirituality of direct experience, either as personal epiphany, *autopsia*, or as mediated by a hierophant, *epopteia*. Notably, the hierophant of the Eleusinian Mysteries dressed as Dionysus, an indicator that these rites involved varieties of ecstatic experience. That the Mysteries offered an alternative to government-sanctioned forms of worship was reason enough for their rigorous persecution. To this day, in countries which ostensibly embrace freedom of religion, many of the elements of the Mystery religions remain outlawed or persecuted: usage of vision-inducing plants and fungi, allegedly aberrant sexual behavior, and controversial forms of music.

*Three Myths*

# THE HORNED GOD

Perhaps such prohibitions explain why Dionysus, the horned god of Nature's bounty and wildness, came to be depicted as the horned devil of folk tales, an image propagated by Christian priests for its usefulness in destroying the ancient religion. Pan suffered similar treatment at the hands of the emerging orthodoxy.

"The lust of the goat is the bounty of God,"[8] William Blake proclaims. While this sentiment may be shocking to many who read it, it is certainly consistent with the ideas of sacred power belonging to the horned god. Whether he sports the horns of a goat, ram, or bull, Dionysus embodies an earthy sexual energy which was vital in the exaltation of initiates and celebrants.

Likewise, the serpents which entwine about the god represent the *kundalini* energy of yoga, that life-force which is said to coil at the root of the spinal column. Shiva, as the Lord of Yoga and the Dionysus of the Hindus, awakens this energy, personified as Shakti. By rousing this serpent-power, he experiences blissful union with the ancient snake-goddess who presides over the powers of the subterranean realm. As the subtle centers of the body, the *chakras*, are energized by the ascent of *kundalini*, the practitioner's body becomes a magical microcosm which contains all of the forces found in the macrocosmic world.

Each of the seven *chakras* or seven heavens has its own system of correspondence and energy patterns. The yogi first experiences the yellow *Muladhara chakra* which is connected with earth energy, the anus, and also the nose. The next subtle center is the white *Svadhishtana chakra*, located at the base of the genitalia and adorned with the half-moon which regulates the sexual life-energy. This *chakra* is associated with the esoteric force of the element of water, the active penis, and the tongue. Above this is the *Manipura chakra*, the fiery red labyrinth of the viscera emblazoned with a swastika. Here the perception of sight is assimilated. Located at the solar plexus is the *Ananhata chakra*, symbolized by the interlocking triangles which form the seal of Solomon. It governs the circulatory system and receives tactile perceptions. *Vishuddha*, the fifth *chakra*, is found in the throat and radiates a brilliant white light. It is connected with the sense of hearing and the element of ether. Sixth in the series is the *Ajna chakra*, the celebrated third eye which relates to the pineal gland. Picturing the spinal column or *sushumna* crowned with the pineal third eye, one may recognize the staff of Dionysus — the pine-cone topped thyrsus. In addition to being the namesake of the pineal gland, the pine-cone is a repository of seeds which are ejected when burned by forest fires, a process which once depended on the intervention of lightning. Not surprisingly, this *chakra* is the color of fire. When the third eye of Shiva is opened, the illusion of the world is obliterated by a thunderbolt. Finally, there is a *Sahasrara chakra* — the thousand-petalled lotus which erupts from the skull-cap, carrying the yogi out of the mundane world. An important clue to the sexual nature of *kundalini* energy is encoded in the image of the snake coiled around Shiva's penis and licking the urethra opening with its forked tongue.

The glyph of the Baphomet, the goat-headed god discussed in an accompanying essay, unites the symbol of the horns with that of the serpent-fire of yogic ecstasy. Esoterically, the horns can be seen as the poles of manifestation: darkness and light, male and female (the Baphomet is hermaphroditic), paradise and creation. Between these horns, jutting from the center of the goat's head, blazes the torch which represents the risen *kundalini* energy. Here is the embodiment of Blake's ideal, the animal energy which paradoxically explodes in heavenly bliss. Author Rene Guenon connects the horns of the god with the linguistic root KRN. This root is found in the word "crown," since the first crowns were adorned with horns. It is also the source of the name Cernunnos, the horned god of the Celts. One may find this root in the name of the city of Karnak in Egypt. Carnival and the corona of the phallus also come to mind. Additionally, it seems probable that this is the root of an important agricultural sacrament associated with Dionysus — the old-world corn identified as barley.

*Three Myths*

# DIONYSUS AS AN AGRICULTURAL DEITY

Corn Dionysus or King Eleusis was the divine child whose arrival was celebrated in the Greater Mysteries of the September harvest. He was the son of a virgin queen, Ogygia, the wise goddess of the sea, who was also known as Calypso or Aphrodite. His arrival was believed to quicken the following year's harvest and he was associated with the bull and other horned animals. Like Moses, Taliesin, and Romulus, the child was found by mystagogues on a river-bank, where he had run aground in his floating winnowing basket, a tool used to separate the barleycorn from the chaff at harvest, the latter of which was blown away by the equinoctial winds. As such, it was an appropriate symbol of the Mysteries, which were open only to the elect few who received them through agricultural parables.

Later, Christianity's emergence placed similar importance on the birth of the miracle child at the time of the Winter Solstice. In fact, the name Eleusis translates to "advent," which consists of Christmas Day and its preceding four weeks. Jesus, speaking in his agricultural parables, could easily be rooted in the ancient Mystery traditions. Just as the twin sacraments of barleycorn and wine were ritually transubstantiated as the flesh and blood of the risen god, so were wheat-wafer and wine regarded in the later Christian Mysteries. What has changed in this transition is the man-god's nature. Although sharing the Dionysian trait of social and theological rebellion, Christ is essentially more mild than wild.

Naturally, the pagan Mysteries differed from Christianity in many significant respects. In one pagan ritual of death and resurrection, the last sheaf of the harvest was cut down and made into a human or animal likeness. With their eyes averted, harvesters spirited this corn-dolly into a barn where it was placed on a shrine until the next planting season. At that time, the figure was carried out and buried in the corn fields to insure a bumper harvest. In this context, the force of Nature was identified and appeased.

## Three Myths

In the Greek and Roman terms for crow, respectively *korone* and *kornix*, the "KRN" indicates that the black bird is a harbinger of the horned god who came to preside over agriculture. The story of the Greek god Kronos being castrated by his son, Zeus, with a scythe contains elements of sexual symbolism mixed with those of the harvest ritual. In such a ritual, the sexual life-energy of the masculine god is sacrificed to the Great Mother Goddess of the Earth in order to provide vitality and crop abundance. His body is then devoured as a sacrament. In Athens, Kronos was identified with Sabazius, another mask of Dionysus. Agriculturally, the harvest of each sheaf of barleycorn corresponds to the castration of the god, associated with the Winter diminution of his powers. This is why such care is taken with the last sheaf of the harvest — why it is personified and returned to the earth prior to planting. There, as a seed, it will fertilize the Earth and return in the Spring.

This ritual emasculation was sometimes carried out literally in the sacred brothels of the goddesses Astarte and Cybele, where ceremonial castration of male priests was practiced for similar reasons. In this sect, Attis was the name of the young vegetation god and son of the goddess. His miraculous birth resulted from the insertion of a pomegranate into the goddess's breast. In the Greek Mysteries, the pomegranate tree was said to sprout in the spilled blood of Dionysus and the eating of its fruit trapped Persephone in the underworld with Hades during the Winter months. In one version of Attis's death, he is said to have autoemasculated himself at the base of a pine tree, his blood nourishing the roots and his spirit returning in the form of this tree.

While most contain sexual symbolism, all agricultural rituals celebrate the all-pervasive universal life-force that is identified with Dionysus as the *Spermatic Logos*. Indeed, one's health and vitality depend on this force for oxygen, sustenance, and shelter. In the preparation of a corn or grain sacrament, there is a recognition that the same life energy informs both human procreation as well as the regeneration of agriculture. This is why the bread is identified with the flesh of the god and the wine with his blood. First, the corn or grain seed of the masculine god is placed in the womb of the mortar where it is ground into

## Three Myths

meal or flour with thrusts and turns of a phallic pestle. Fluids sacred to the feminine goddess are then added — milk, oil, or water — and the mixture is churned in a reenactment of sexual congress. Living yeast is added and the dough is placed in darkness where it will rise until the time comes to place it in the transforming womb of the hot oven.

In eating such a sacrament and drinking the wine-blood of the god (fermentation is a process as mysterious as preparing the bread sacrament), there is a shift in emphasis from human or animal sacrifice to that of the god in vegetation form. Sparagmos, the reenactment of Dionysus' dismemberment, gives way to the harvest trials and death of Corn-Dionysus or John Barleycorn. As a result of this symbolic shift, more emphasis is placed on the aspect of the god as a deity of vegetation — the mysterious Green Man who appears in a variety of forms.

In *The Secret Teachings of All Ages*, Manly P. Hall recounts the Masonic legend of the master builder of Solomon's Temple, Hiram Abiff. The tale of his fate is yet another version of the story of the dying and resurrecting harvest-god, John Barleycorn. Just as Hiram Abiff is murdered by three renegade fellow-craft Masons, John Barleycorn is brought down by three men from the West who have taken the solemn vow that John Barleycorn or "Little Sir John" must die. As the Spring gives way to Summer and Autumn, Little Sir John grows a beard (begins to bear grain) and becomes a mature man. His fate is to be harvested. He will be decapitated, wheeled around and around, and his body will be torn to pieces, year after year. John Barleycorn's body serves as a dual sacrament, being prepared as both sustaining bread and intoxicating beer. His three assassins are the three months of Winter, during which Little Sir John dwells in the underworld. This is the time when it is said that the Green Man sleeps, to awaken again when Spring erupts in its bounty. Little Sir John is also characterized as Little John in the Robin Hood myths that we will examine later.

*Three Myths*

# DIONYSUS AS SACRED PHALLUS AND SPERMATIC LOGOS

The ubiquitous force of the *Spermatic Logos* is identified with Dionysus. It is the vehicle through which celebrants enjoy firsthand experience of the reality of the god. Just as a practitioner of the Voodoo religion are temporarily inhabited or "ridden" by Loas (the gods of the Afro-Caribbean faith), so is the celebrant of Dionysus exalted as the living presence of the god. Such an experience is a living furnace of transgression, bridging the gap between polarities. Dissolving the barriers between God and man, man and beast, tradition and taboo, Dionysus spreads from heart to burning heart, threatening to destroy and recreate the world. This wild god of the forest crouches, ready to spring, concealed only by the tall grasses of the brain's right hemisphere. Ithyphallic satyrs and voluptuous maenads dance in his party — an other-worldly traveling carnival which leaves bliss in its wake and inverts the usual social order. The god interpenetrates the minds and souls the celebrants and fills them with divine fire.

> Yes, I know from where I came!
> Ever hungry like a flame,
> I consume myself and glow.
> Light grows all that I conceive,
> Ashes everything I leave:
> Flame I am assuredly.[9]

This symbolic fire is the voice of the *Spermatic Logos*, a force also known as the Generative Reason and the Green Man of Knowledge. As characterized by Dionysus, it is Phleus, the Abundance of Life. The form of the god in which this force resides is known as Dendrite, that name of Dionysus which means "of the Tree" and also refers to the branching fractals of brain cells. In Sumerian, GEShTIN is both the Tree of Life and "vine", the latter being the emblem of both Dionysus and Jesus.

Dead Sea Scrolls translator and scholar John M. Allegro identifies this force as both IA-U-ShU-A, the Sumerian root of Jesus, and IA-U-NU-ShUSh, Dionysus. Both of these names mean "semen, that saves and restores," a reference to the pure seminal fluid of the god. Similarly, the name of one of Shiva's sons, Skanda, means "jet of sperm." As the characteristic energy of this semen changes depending on the sacrament of the god, it can produce sustenance, fertility, and even divine intoxication. For example, this seminal energy is thought by many cultures to reside within the sap and flesh of "entheogenic" healing and psychoactive plants.[10] Allegro even makes a convincing linguistic case that the early Christian Mysteries were celebrated with a sacrament of visionary mushroom bread.

Accordingly, Shiva/ Dionysus/ Cernunnos frequently appears in symbol and in manifestation as the erect penis, the home of the god's priapic energy and the locus of erotic and sacred bliss. Meaning "Happiness Dwells Here," the phrase *Htc Habitat Felicitas* was a legend frequently emblazoned below the totem phallus found in many Roman households. In the monthlong rites of Liberalia, a precursor of the old European Mayday festivities, the enormous likeness of an erect penis was paraded throughout the village marketplace amidst wild celebration. In a fertility ceremony evocative of sexual union, an honored matron would put the excited phallus to rest by fitting a wreath onto it. While in the Celtic religion the phallus survived as Jack in the Green, thrusting skyward as an enormous, leafy phallus, its head ejaculating an orgasmic spray of flowers from a masked face into a floral wreath. This complex symbol is also a form of the Tree of Life — the *axis mundi* or center of the world.

Liberalia was similar to the Greek Dionysia Festival and to the Lenea, the great feast of the wine-presses. Dionysus was represented as a rigid phallus and honored by drinking, dancing, singing, sex, and practical jokes. The observance of the latter was undoubtedly part of the origin of modern April Fool's Day. Spring was also the time of the Elaphebolion, the City Dionysia. In parts of Greece, these rites were celebrated solely by women

## Three Myths

who, clad in goatskins, ascended the peaks of certain mountains where they would play frenzied music, enjoy an excess of intoxicants, dance and indulge in a sapphic, orgiastic crescendo.

One of the myths of the Hindu god Shiva, the Dionysus of India, sheds light on this identification of the deity with the phallus, the symbol of the creative principle in Nature. Worshippers of Shiva revere the phallus or *linga* as the source of divine pleasure, a state called *ananda*, and commune with their lord through a non-reproductive erotic ecstasy. Many practice a bliss-inducing sexual yoga called *tantra*. By regulating mental activity and meditating, the faithful seek knowledge of an interior, subtle *linga*. "Shiva said, 'I am not distinct from the phallus. The phallus is identical with me. It draws my faithful to me, and therefore must be worshipped. My well-beloved! Wherever there is an upright male organ, I myself am present, even if there is no other representation of me."[11]

In the *Skanda Purana*, Shiva is cursed by sages who do not recognize the god, causing his penis to drop off. In the form of his own gigantic *linga*, Shiva penetrates the three worlds and proceeds to terrorize everyone, burning whatever is in his path. The monster phallus burrows into the underworld, and even ascends to heaven to wreak havoc. The Shiva *linga* appears to be unstoppable. In despair, the sages appeal to the god Brahma, who directs them to construct a great vagina with which to placate the organ. After lubricating the big, crazy penis with holy water, the sages sing to it, play music for it, pray, chant, and finally thrust it into the happy place — the vagina of the Lady of the Mountain, Shiva's consort.

Here again is the curse of Dionysus. Those who thwart his ways and persecute him are condemned to madness and destruction.

## Three Myths

The Dionysian energy and wildness must be put to use generating ecstatic bliss. For if it is repressed, it will demand expression in violence and its madness will be the seed of destruction. Sexual repression fails to harness the life-force and, on a mass scale, it results in fascism, as the revolutionary psychotherapist Wilhelm Reich demonstrated. Reich based his therapies on the idea that there is a flowing life energy, something that he called *orgone*. A perfect image for this *orgone*, the energy of the *Spermatic Logos* is Andre Masson's drawing of Acéphale, whose decapitated head is fixed over his *linga*. On one level, this headless figure is the symbol of an egalitarian collective — an organization or society without an authoritarian head. But to the Greeks, the head was the head of barleycorn which Plato referred to as "the image of the world." This head of barleycorn was also the central symbol of the Eleusinian Mysterics — the world, nourishment, the flesh of the god, the seed as a unit of life energy.

In Hindu tradition, the severed head that Kali holds aloft is said to transform into Shiva's severed yet erect *linga* — the conduit for *ananda*, sacred erotic bliss. As such, it will burst up from the underworld to penetrate the thousand-petalled lotus. Tantrically, the conjunction of the head and the penis would seem to represent the bliss of the *urdhvareta*, one whose sexual energy has rocketed up from the genitals to blossom in or above the head, as when it manifests as the *sahasrara chakra* and its multi-petalled lotus. In such a case, the head — the seat of reason — is informed and inflamed by the sexual life-force, the *kundalini*.

Perhaps this conjunction of head and phallus is a clue to the esoteric nature of the Green Man — known in Islam as Khidr, a prophet and initiator. The ejaculating face of the Jack in the Green, as we have seen, converges with a huge, leafy, ithyphallic penis. Other variations of the Green Man show him as a head disgorging leaves and vines from his mouth — an orgasmic spasm of springtime, regeneration of the *Sper-*

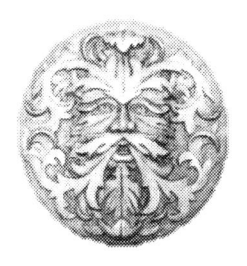

*matic Logos*. Dionysus appears in many sacramental forms in the botanical world — as the miracle of fermentation and wine, the god's intoxicating blood; as the fertile seed of sowing and the dismemberment of reaping; and as psychoactive plant sacraments. All plants contain this all-pervasive force of nature characterized as the Green Man of cathedral architecture and folk tales. And the Green Man, in turn, can be found behind a typically Dionysian assortment of masks.

# ROBIN HOOD

While the Green Man presents us with a crucial aspect of the god, the wild deity of the woods known as Robin Hood may give us a better idea of his multi-faceted nature. Robin Hood was said to be an outlaw who made his home in the forests and wild places. As a spirit of the woods, he was also known as Robin Goodfellow or Puck. With his merry band, he is known to have haunted Sherwood Forest in Nottinghamshire, forcibly redistributing wealth from those with plenty to sadly impoverished souls. But as Puck, dramatized in *A Midsummer Night's Dream* by William Shakespeare, the figure is a visitor from the land of the *sidhe* — the realm of the Good People or fairies.

> Either I mistake your shape and making quite
> Or else you are that shrewd and knavish sprite
> Call'd Robin Goodfellow: are you not he
> That frights the maidens of the villagery;
> Skim milk, and sometimes labour in the quern
> And bootless make the breathless housewife churn;
> And sometime make the drink to bear no barm;
> Mislead night-wanderers, laughing at their harm?
> Those that Hobgoblin call you and sweet Puck,
> You do their work, and they shall have good luck.[12]

Robin Goodfellow's bawdy rites were celebrated by 16th and 17th century groups of traveling gypsy players who performed their rituals throughout the British Isles, disguising them as plays. In these traditions, we see a continuation of many significant elements of the religion of Shiva/Dionysus: sacred drama, a god who travels in the company of unearthly beings, and the sexuality common to Hindu *tantra* and Dionysian revel.

## Three Myths

These banned plays were revived by Scottish Lord Justice General Sir William Sinclair, a Freemason who hosted an annual gypsy revel which was held each May and June at his family estate of Rosslyn. The chapel of Rosslyn was even garlanded with sculptures of vines sprouting from the mouths of a multitude of Green Men. These performing gypsies were housed in two towers of the estate which became known as "Robin Hood" and "Little John," perhaps a symbolic form of the two pillars of Masonic ritual. Their play included characters such as the Abbot of Unreason, identified with Friar Tuck of the Robin Hood legends, and the Queen of the May, Maid Marion.

According to Michael Baigent and Richard Leigh in *The Temple and the Lodge*:

> The Robin Hood legend provided, in effect, a handy guise whereby the fertility rites of ancient paganism were introduced back into the bosom of nominally Christian Britain. Every May Day there would be a festival of unabashedly pagan origin. Rituals would be enacted around the 'May Pole,' traditional symbol of the archaic goddess of sexuality and fertility. On Midsummer's Day, every village virgin would become, metaphorically, Queen of the May. Many of them would be ushered into the 'Greenwood' where they would undergo their sexual initiation at the hands of a youth playing Robin Hood or Robin Goodfellow, while Friar Tuck, the 'Abbot of Unreason,' would officiate, blessing the mating couples in a parody of formal nuptials. By virtue of such role-playing, the borders separating dramatic masque and fertility ritual would effectively dissolve. May Day would be, in fact, a day of orgy. Nine months later, it would produce, throughout the British Isles, its annual crop of children. It was in these 'sons of Robin' that many such family names as Robinson and Robertson first originated.[13]

## Three Myths

Poet Robert Graves connects the character of Robin Hood to Merddin or Merlin, known to the Saxons as *Rof Breoht Woden*, the "Bright Strength of Woden." Graves describes a revealing image from a pamphlet published in 1639, *Robin Goodfellow, his mad pranks and merry jests:* "Robin is depicted as an ithyphallic god of the witches with young ram's horns sprouting from his forehead, ram's legs, a witches' besom over his left shoulder, a lighted candle in his right hand. Behind him in a ring dance a coven of men and women witches in Puritan costume, a black dog adores him, a musician plays a trumpet, an owl flies overhead … in Cornwall "Robin" means phallus."[14] To those who told the tales of Robin Hood, he was a symbol of freedom — the old horned god of the forest rising up against the Roman-Christian invaders.

His consort Marion takes the form of the ancient goddess of the sea and love, known variously as Marian, the mermaid, Calypso, Aphrodite — whose name means "risen from the sea foam" — and *Stilla Maris*, the Virgin Mary who is the "Myrrh of the Sea." Her temples were often adorned with sea-shells and other treasures from the deep, just as her rites were connected with water. "Every initiate of the Eleusinian Mysteries, which were of Pelasgian origin, went through a love rite with her representative after taking a cauldron bath…"[15]

As "Mary Gipsy" or St. Mary of Egypt, she is also the patroness of poets and lovers. Graves wryly notes that St. Mary booked her passage to the Holy Land by offering her services as a prostitute to the crew of the only vessel sailing there. She then spent years as a desert anchorite and after her death was supposed to offer special indulgence to those committing carnal sins. As an allegory, St. Mary of Egypt can be seen as a characterization of the temple prostitutes of dynastic Egypt, ancient Greece, and fallen Babylon. She would have regarded sexual intercourse as a sacrament, an integral part of the *hieros gamos* or sacred marriage, ferrying the devout across the Great Waters in her boat of heaven. Graves speculates that the sect of Mary Gipsy was encountered by the Crusaders in the Holy Land. Celebrants of the sect lived there under the protection of the Moslems, who supposedly wooed them from orthodoxy. From there, the faith was carried to Compostella, Spain by pilgrims and invading Moors.

From Spain, it was adopted by troubadours who spread it as the religion of courtly love — earthly romance and union as the manifestation of divine love, the *fideli d'amor*.

The dusky-faced Moors who appeared in fertility festivals of the British Isles were perhaps vectors of Middle Eastern Sufism, a mystical aspect of Islam which passed through the doorway of Spain into Western culture. In *The Sufis*, Idries Shah speculates that the Aniza Bedouin were the source of medieval witchcraft as it appeared in the West, a remnant of more arcane rituals. Indeed, the wild god seems to be present in Islam as a revered prophet, as we shall soon see.

At this point, it is interesting to consider the initiations of these Moors, the dancing Morris Men. As musicians serenade them, the Morris Dancers pass through the arch of a doorway, formed by the group's captain holding his wooden phallus-staff against the Maypole. Meanwhile dancers, clowns, a hobby-horse, and a fool whirl about them. Next, the Morris Men lie face-down on the ground as the dancers leap over them and clowns prod them on the buttocks. These soot-blackened clowns caper about the pole with makeshift phallic wands, thrusting their hips lewdly at participants and spectators alike. Finally, the black-faced Morris Men are beaten on the soles of their feet with staves, many struggling to escape the punishment phase of the ritual. After this, there is a march around the Maypole as dancers cry, "Calu-Sar!" As marching gives way to dancing, the martial strains are drowned out by a rapid, vibrating sound, the psycho-acoustic effects of which we will examine later. This jig is said to be a medicine dance, one that infuses energy into the participants and the community.

## THE FOOL, THE SIGNIFYING MONKEY, AND KHIDR

Who is the Fool of the Mayday ritual and Morris Dance, the madly wise counselor to kings? In the Tarot deck — or as the Joker in the modern deck of cards — the Fool is set apart from the other Trumps and is designated by the number zero. In spirit, he is none other than Dionysus himself, as is evident from his rites and travails. Clad in colorful rags and motley, the Fool capers, sings, lampoons, and makes merry. And at the climax of his mad dance, he dies and is resurrected. As an advisor to kings, the Fool offers his counsel couched in lampoon, song, and crazy wisdom.

In British Christmastide dramas, the Fool is the central figure who represents the head of a secret society composed of black-faced members, undoubtedly the Morris Men. These members or "sons" must kill the Fool, the head of their house. As he dies and descends into the underworld, he carries all of the misfortunes and tribulations of the prior year with him. When he returns, resurrected, he is the rejuvenated leader who is ready to meet the challenges of the forthcoming year. In some folk plays, the Fool is killed by six sword-dancers, six being a number associated with the sun. After he has died, been resurrected, and has regaled the crowd with tales of his adventures beyond the grave, the Fool competes with his eldest son for the love of the hermaphroditic Lady. She is a symbol of the union of opposites which is also found in *Tantra*. In this one figure, the femininity of space and the masculinity of time combine. It can also be seen as the dynamic masculine force fertilizing feminine matter. At the source of such a union, a vibration or sound begins, which creates the substance of the universe. The Fool wins this Lady and a wild round of dancing ensues.

Like the god of the woods, the Fool may perform as some creature of the animal world, wearing skins and masks while capering and performing bestial antics. Or he may appear as the Leafy Fool, an embodiment of the potencies found in the plant world. In either case, he is considered foolish only because he is attuned to the world of Nature. Because of this, his wisdom may not be readily perceived by representatives of civilization and its light.

In Portugal, the Fool leads a dancing company of crude, masked "monkeys," or *Bugios,* who are similar to the Morris Dancers. And, like the pattern in a dance, these monkeys revel and reveal themselves to be simian variants of Shiva/ Dionysus. In a biography of the Arabian explorer, Sufi, and mystic Sir Richard

## Three Myths

Burton, Byron Farwell claimed that his subject lived with a company of monkeys:

> Deciding that monkeys were preferable to his messmates, Burton collected about forty of various breeds and proceeded to live with them — but in a civilized manner, of course. He assigned them ranks and titles and formed his own mess. He taught them to sit at the table and had servants wait on them. Beside him sat a tiny, pretty, silky-looking monkey he called his wife. As a final touch he put pearls in her ears. The monkeys became involved in his language studies and he began to form a simian vocabulary. Using his usual system, he repeated the sounds of the monkeys until he could imitate them and claimed to have collected about sixty 'leading words'.[16]

Though his contemporaries would have scoffed at his conversational efforts with his hairy friends, scientists today agree that trans-simian communication is a limited reality. There has always existed a kinship between humans and so-called "lesser" or "lower" primates. Religious fundamentalism in the West would have us believe that humans are entirely distinct from apes and monkeys, but a mere glance at the numerous genotypical similarities suggests some kind of evolutionary link, whether one subscribes to Darwinism or not. Non-European cultures have a better understanding of the relationship between man and monkey. To such cultures, the monkey is not only a mirror of humanity, but also the embodiment of the playful aspects of divinity.

For instance, the Hindu faith emphasizes the importance of monkeys by including one in their complex pantheon, as the following myth explains. One day Shiva became so aroused at the sight of Vishnu in the form of the beautiful enchantress Mohini, he ejaculated. Seven quick-thinking sages caught the divine jism on a leaf and poured it into the ear of Anjani, the daughter of Gautama. As a result of this odd experiment, Anjani became pregnant and thereafter delivered a bouncing baby monkey-god. Named Hanuman, this incarnation of the wild god Shiva was so impetuous that he would have eaten the sun like a ripe piece of fruit, if the gods had not begged him to stop. In the *Ramayana*, Hanuman performs many miraculous acts to help reunite the lovers Rama and Sita. Many depictions of Hanuman show the trickster monkey-god carrying a mountain of healing herbs to a battlefield to resurrect his monkey friends who have been slain by demons.

Visions of sacred monkeys occur to this day. Author Jean Houston was rescued from a horrifying di-methyltryptamine experience by a sudden vision of a monkey-sage. And the monkey-god Hanuman continues to receive praise and veneration, as well. In 1997, hot-air balloonist Steve Fossett had to stop his around-the-world flight short of his goal, setting down in Nunkhar, India. His arrival was greeted with amazement by villagers who thought that the second coming of the divine simian Hanuman was upon them, and that the monkey-god was landing in a space-station temple.

In African folktales there is the figure of the Signifying Monkey who taunts and lampoons the Jungle King, tricking his way out of each fix. Another African tradition claims that all monkeys are capable of speech, but will never let on, knowing that human beings would put them to work. Whether strictly identified with Shiva or Dionysus, the monkeys of myth and folktale seem to universally partake of the god's trickster aspect and his untamed nature.

The archetype of the sacred monkey is also found in China in the epic folklore cycle *Journey to the West*. Great Sage Equal to Heaven is the brash and prankish Monkey King who raids the peach orchards of Heaven, then steals and drinks the elixir of immortality from the sage Lao Tsu. Curiously, a magical girdle figures prominently in the adventures of the Chinese Monkey King, just as it does in the story of Sir Gawain in his confrontation with the Green Knight. In one legend of St. George — the saint identified with the Green Man — the girdle becomes an interesting symbol, in that it relates the Green Man to the powers of his goddess consort. In ancient Greece, the Cestus —

## Three Myths

Aphrodite's magic girdle — was a symbol of love and fertility. Green and gold, the colors of this girdle, stand for, respectively, life energy and spiritual perfection.

The mysterious prophet of Islam, known as Khidr, has been identified with the Green Man, too. Considering the contact between the ancient Greek civilization and the Middle East, the possibility exists that Dionysus was transplanted into esoteric Islam. The practice of trance-inducing dances among dervishes and the spiritual symbol of wine and divine intoxication in Sufi poetry seem remarkably similar to the praxis of Dionysiac traditions. Khidr is identified as a prophet who may appear to the masterless or natural Sufi in a dream, vision, or spiritual encounter, as he did to the Great Sheikh Ibn Arabi. In the Koran, Khidr is associated with both Moses and Alexander the Great, even while serving as a bridge between esoteric Islam and the Mystery Schools:

> During the ceremonies of initiation into the Ancient Mysteries, it is supposed that the neophyte left the physical body in a trance state, and in full consciousness, which he retained afterwards, entered the subjective world and beheld all its wonders and inhabitants; and that coming out of that world he was clothed in a robe of sacred green to symbolize his own spiritual resurrection and re-birth into real life — for he had penetrated the Mystery of Death and was now an initiate. Even yet there seems to be an echo of the ancient Egyptian Mysteries in the Festival of Al-Khidr celebrated in the middle of the wheat harvest in lower Egypt. Al-Khidr is a holy personage who, according to the belief of the people, was the vizier of Dhu'l-Karnen [the KRN of this name seems to etymologically link him to the horned deity in one of his facets], a contemporary of Abraham, and who, never having died, is still living and will continue to live until the Day of Judgement. And he is always represented 'clad in green garments, whence probably the name' he bears. Green is thus associated with a hero or god who is immortal and un-

changing like the Tuatha De Danann and fairy races...In modern Masonry, which preserves many of the ancient mystic rites, and to some extent those of initiation as anciently performed, green is the symbol of life, immutable nature, of truth, and victory. In the evergreen acacia [identified by Robert Graves with the burning bush beheld by Moses], the Master Mason finds the emblem of hope and immortality. And the Masonic authority who gives this information suggests that in all the Ancient Mysteries this symbolism was carried out — green symbolizing the birth of the world and the moral creation or resurrection of the initiate."[17]

It should be noted that the symbol of the fish is common to both Khidr and Jesus Christ, that latter of whom is sometimes referred to as the Fish. Representing fecundity, a fish carries the green-clad Khidr across the River of Life. The fish is also one of Shiva's tantric sacraments, a representation of the vagina in sexual yoga. Elsewhere it is considered a phallic symbol.

## PART TWO: UNDERGROUND

There is much in Christianity to suggest that it is an extension of the Dionysian Mysteries, rather than strictly being the offspring of Judaism. Dionysus and Christ have much in common. They were both divine sons delivered by mortal women who had been miraculously impregnated by God the Father — Yahweh or Zeus. The sacrament of both Dionysus and Jesus is wine, which is ritually consumed as transubstantiated blood, and wheat baked into bread, the god's flesh. Like Dionysus, Jesus was tolerant and welcomed prostitutes and outcasts into his circle. Both were sacrificed. Both rose again. And each promises that he will return to initiate a new golden age.

Many of the branches of the Christian faith have yielded fruit of sublime beauty, as well as hybridizations with other religions. Both inside and outside the channels of orthodoxy, countless Christians have distinguished themselves in gentleness of spirit

## Three Myths

and breathtaking acts of love and charity. Theosophical Christians — who sought the experience of Sophia, the feminine wisdom of esoteric Christianity — conceived of mystical approaches to the Christian faith which gave it an experiential depth beyond the boundaries of orthodoxy. And, as evidenced by the *Divine Comedy* of Dante among other artistic works, Christianity even contained currents of the *fedeli d'amore*, the tendency to regard one's beloved as a reflection of divine truth and beauty. In such variations, the Kingdom of God is sought within the worshipper through contemplation of symbols found in the world of Nature. Sophia, the Virgin of Wisdom, was once revered by Christians, Sufis, and Jewish Cabalists as a figure representing a true internal state.

But, other aspects of Christianity can only be seen as the cunning, brutal manipulation of worldly power. In such hands, this faith of divine love and forgiveness can become a distorted instrument of murder and persecution. Forged in an alliance between the Roman Empire and the early Christian Church, this hybrid amassed land and wealth through aggressive domestic and foreign Crusades. Novelist Phillip K. Dick refers to this unholy union as "the Empire" or "the Black Iron Prison," a force which he claims continues to dominate human beings. Its spread is due to the mechanisms of fear and guilt. Those who think to oppose it or attempt to live outside of its context tend to be marginalized as sinners or Satanists. Accordingly, many have been murdered.

In the course of time, the old religion and its rituals were subverted in the West and recontextualized by Christian priests. Some Irish pagans claimed that these priests came to curse the land. Sacred temples, monuments, and land were seized from the pagans, cleared, and used as sites for Christian churches. By laminating their holy days over the festivals of existing folk traditions, the Christian priests sought to usurp the ancient religion. And in many cases, Yahweh, Mary, and Christ were accepted as new forms of familiar deities. But there were some notable differences between Christ and the horned god of the pagans. For example, even as late as the 18th century, Christians were still arguing bitterly as to whether Jesus had ever laughed. This was a far cry from the mad, prankish forest god, just as the dourness and guilt of Christianity (relieved by the occasional mirthful exception such as St. Francis) was alien to practitioners of the ancient religion. The practice of paganism — or any unauthorized variant form of Christianity for that matter — was condemned as demonic and heretical.

Constantine, the first Roman emperor to convert to Christianity, regarded Jesus as an incarnation of the sun god. During his reign, the practice of Christianity became legal, but as this faith fused with the Roman Empire, it soon became the state religion. For a time it was the only legal faith, which was used by the Roman government as an instrument of oppression. As the political machinations of the Empire rolled forward, variant forms of the Christian faith, such as Gnosticism, were targeted and forcibly eradicated. Nevertheless, this very attempt at earthly conquest exposed Christians to new theologies and systems of thought. "Holy" wars such as the Crusades provided points of contact between cultures and faiths. Hybrid idea-forms, like the sect of St. Mary in Egypt, began to appear at the unpoliced outer limits of the Empire, sometimes going unchecked and unpunished for years. As soon as the Christian religion was adopted as the tool of Empire. Teaching that life was a veil of tears and human beings were sinful by nature, Christian priests focused the attention of the populace on the reward of the afterlife. Misery and sin were one's lot. Heaven was the reward of docile spirits who repented their sins and submitted to rule by the Christian invaders. The virtues of humility and meekness in the populace were not overlooked as advantages to a burgeoning Empire.

It was not long before the prankish horned god donned the mask of this new religion. Practices sacred to Dionysus began to appear in the context of the Christian faith, possibly as a result of the many similarities between these two sons of God. For instance, the heretical 14th century Brethren of the Free Spirit celebrated a unique interpretation of Christian doctrine which seemed to have more in common with the traditions of the wild god of fertility than with Christ.

## *Three Myths*

Free Spirit John Hartmann, slain by the Inquisition in 1368, identified Mary Magdalene as an inspiration to Free Spirit theology. According to Hartmann, the possible sexual involvement of Jesus with Mary Magdalene was the subject of serious research by the sect. From his confession, one may see not only a survival of Dionysian forms of worship, but also an anticipation of the attitude of Acéphale and other "radical" 20th century thinkers. Hartmann stated that it was not only lawful to grant the body what it wanted, but that "those who are in this degree of perfection and in the freedom of spirit are no longer obliged to obey men, or any precept, or the rules of the Church: they are truly free. Such a man is king and master of all creatures. Everything belongs to him. He may legitimately receive whatever he likes and take it for his own use. And if anyone should prevent him, to put an obstacle in his way or seize his possessions, he would be justified in killing him. By putting him to death, he would be returning him to his original element. He may legitimately undertake anything that ensures his pleasure."[18] Furthermore, Hartmann incited, it would be a better thing for the whole world to perish than for a celebrant of the Free Spirit to renounce an urge imparted by Nature.

Celebrants of the Free Spirit responded to this idea by claiming to be without sin and enjoying sacramental sex. Paradise was to be experienced in the moment, they believed. Regarding the orthodox Church as an earthly empire that was tricking people in a kind of cosmic shell-game, the Free Spirits denounced this institution and its power over their lives. Many of them were murdered by the Empire as a result. This tactic proved very useful in extinguishing competitive sects in the early history of the Roman-Christian church.

A sensationalist writer named John of Winterthur first chronicled the lusty excesses of the Free Spirit sect, an account which made his readers sick with revulsion. How many of these excesses sprang from his own fevered brain is unknown. The questionably extracted "confessions" of three members of this sect included some of the sect's beliefs: a Pantheistic conviction that God was in everything (or, as John of Winterthur would explain

## Three Myths

it, there is as much divine goodness in a louse as there is in a man); a rejection of communion as food for pigs; and, most importantly, the idea that sexual intercourse on an altar was the *real* consecration of the host. In one story, three women sought the knowledge of a Brother of the Free Spirit who promptly stripped them, sexually satisfied them, and then proclaimed, "here is the Holy Trinity!" Far from mere blasphemy, this statement alluded to sexual mysticism as a method for achieving spiritual ends.

Inspired by the 13th century mystic Meister Eckhart (charged with heresy for statements like "As God penetrates me, I penetrate God in return"), the Free Spirits sought to live without a rule and to serve God through the "liberty of the spirit." Mechthild of Megdeburg, a female Free Spirit (or *Beguine*) wrote in her *Flowing Light of the Godhead*: "Thou art in me and I in Thee." This was an early expression of bride mysticism, called *Minnemystik*, which equated God with sexual rapture. But, far from objective, the outraged John of Winterthur was more obsessed with sensational tales of Austrian orgies. In one such account, an aphrodisiacal grasshopper leapt into the mouth of one celebrant, sparking a wild orgy.

This fertile soil surely gave rise the ideas of Jacob Boehme, a 16th century German mystic who saw a "great secret" in the sex drive. Males and females, Boehme argued, tormented by separation into two from the androgynous Adam, lusted after their opposites. Within the will, he went on, longing for unity and completion was sexual. Base lust contained the formula for something higher, that is, eternal light and flight from death and darkness. But simple, blind, procreative sex could never attain the "paradisiacal child of love." Resurrection represents the completion of a greater union of male and female into one being of divine androgyny. Dionysus was sometimes represented as such a being, a living reconciliation of contraries. This process may be accomplished within the body/ soul complex of a single individual, making it one of the keys to Alchemy.

Perhaps the culmination of this current was the philosophy of the 18th century esoteric Christian, Novalis (Friedrich von

*Three Myths*

Hardenburg). Like the Brethren of the Free Spirit, Novalis viewed sexual intercourse as the act of communion: "But whosoever has sucked from hot, beloved lips the breath of life, whose heart has melted in quivering waves under holy blaze, whose eyes opened to measure the unfathomable depth of heaven shall eat of his body and drink of his blood eternally."[19] A student of medicine and physics, he viewed Christianity as "the religion of sensuality." Like the Pantheist Free Spirits, he saw all of creation as partaking of the divine. And in this case, anything could serve as a mediator between man and God. "One should seek God among men...there is but one temple in the world, the human body. Nothing is more sacred than this noble shape...We touch heaven when we run our fingers over a human body."[20] Christ's blood, in Novalis' poetry and prose, stands as a metaphor for the ubiquitous life-force, as when he writes, "in heavenly blood the blessed couple swims."[21] For Novalis and his philosophy, true freedom springs from this ecstatic sexual union.

Freedom, Novalis tells us, erupts from spontaneous passion and revelry. "When numbers and figures/ Are no longer the key to all creatures,/ When those who sing and kiss/ Know more than the deeply learned/ When the world reverts to free life/ And to a free word.../ Then one single secret word/ Will blow away this whole misbegotten mode of existence."[22] Love is liberation, a secret of Nature glimpsed in the vision of a simple blue cornflower. And it is love expressed in sexual union between a man and a woman that crashes through all of the barriers of what we perceive as reality, leaving only bliss in its wake. Sensual delight becomes a vehicle of transcendence, a belief shared by Hindu and Buddhist tantric practitioners. "Order is no longer spatial and temporal/ Here future is in the past./ Love's empire is open..."[23]

Like William Butler Yeats, William Blake, and Robert Graves, Novalis equates the ability to write genuine poetry with the transcendent experience. When one forms a connection to the world soul, art blossoms from the human spirit. But the poet is merely the medium through which language operates. And language behaves much like mathematical formulae. Words, he

## Three Myths

says, "form a world of their own, they play only with themselves, express nothing but their own wonderful nature...just because of this they mirror the strange interplay of objects."[24] From the experience of ecstatic bliss, words rearrange themselves into dynamic abstractions, demanding expression. Conversely, by manipulating words and their values, one may seek to influence this "strange interplay of objects" as in invocation or evocation. And as the *Spermatic Logos* breathes vitality into creation, words and symbols remain as energetic messengers which pass through the illusive subject/ object boundaries of the consciousness.

While examining the legacy of the Free Spirit, one may begin to see the created world as yet another abstraction, or symbol, in which all opposites seek to unite with each other. This act results in a synergetic divine third, that might be perceived as a sacred trinity. This third force is Love in its most mysterious aspect. Love speaks through the dynamic interplay of polarized forces just as the rose blossoms when earth/ air/ fire/ and water are brought into active balance. So in that moment of orgasm, lovers experience the act of creation in reverse; duality becomes unity which is swallowed by the void, the zero of the Fool. The rapture of the flesh feeds the rapture of the spirit. Each lover *becomes* the object of his/ her desire, and the beloved is the very embodiment of everything divine. Sexual union or even the extreme yearning of separated lovers contains the formula for transcendence, a tradition of the *fedeli d'amore*.

To the Roman-Christian church, such theology was appalling and sinful. In order to destroy this ideology before it spread any further, the Church began to torture and murder the Free Spirits. Persecution of "witches" — celebrants of the old Nature religion — resulted in a great human toll, too, since the accused were compelled to either recant their beliefs or be brutally murdered. The old horned god was cunningly recast as a devil, if not as the Prince of Darkness himself. Without any choice in the matter, pagan celebrants were decried as Satanists by their oppressors, much as Jews, Gypsies, and other designated scapegoats were later treated by Nazi invaders in the 20th century. Confronted by the domination of Empire, pagan religions and "heretical" Christian sects were driven underground, their wisdom preserved by secret societies and in the world of art and symbol, as in Alchemy.

## DIONYSIAN SECRET SOCIETIES AND DRAMA AS RITUALIZATION

Acéphale was not the first reported Dionysian secret society. According to occult tradition, there was another, far more ancient secret society associated with the reverence of Dionysus. Its arcane knowledge encrypted into stone, it sought harmony with Nature through study and implementation of sacred geometry, the reflection in Creation of God's divine plan. These Dionysian Artificers were held to be initiates of the Mysteries of Dionysus who held a mystical view of the unity between the universe and its Creator, and sought to express this through construction of temples. Their religious buildings were supposedly intended to represent the human body as a microcosm of the universe.

In *Speculative Masonry*, A.S. Macbride, J.P. points out the similarities between the Dionysian Architects and speculative Freemasons: "that they were distinguished by the exercise of charity; by being divided into Lodges governed by Masters and Wardens; by employing within their ceremonies many of the implements of the Craft; and by having a universal language which served to distinguish a brother in the dark as well as in the light, and which united them over India, Persia, and Syria. At the time of the building of King Solomon's Temple at Jerusalem the existence of this Fraternity in Tyre...'is universally admitted, and Hiram, the widow's son...was doubtless one of its members.'"[25]

These Dionysian Architects are said to have preserved their spirituality in stone — living stone, as it were. It is alleged that they believed that creation and constructiveness were primary expressions of the soul, and, that by acting in accord with the creative aspects of Nature, they could achieve immortality. Additionally, they held that their architecture would awaken mystical and psychological reactions, even among the uninitiated.

Their theory of architecture was based on the Hermetic philosophy and the pantheistic pagan belief in the unity between the universe and God. They also promoted the political idea of Utopia on Earth which was expressed in symbolic form. Humanity was the crude block of stone which the master mason or Grand Architect (God) was constantly molding and polishing to transform it into an object of perfection. The hammer and chisel of the mason became the cosmic forces which shaped the spiritual destiny of humankind. In eighteenth-century speculative Masonry the hammer or gavel was a symbol of divine power. It was used to measure the hallowed precincts of the lodge which was as far as the Grand Master could throw the hammer in any direction.

The Roman architect and Master builder Vitrivius, who was born in the first century C.E., was influenced by the Dionysian Artificers. His theories formed the basis for the architecture of the Roman Empire and, with the rediscovery of classical knowledge in the 16th century, also had an impact on the greatest architects of the Renaissance. Vitrivius' concept of the magical theater representing the microcosmos of the world as a symbol of the macrocosmos of the universe was repeated in William Shakespeare's famous phrase 'All the world's a stage, and all the men and women merely players...' and the naming of his theatre The Globe. It is claimed that Shakespeare was a Rosicrucian initiate and as such would have been familiar with the ideas of Vitrivius and the Dionysian Artificers."[26]

Such lore should not always be taken literally, as historical fact. These stories may simply provide a creative bridge between modern and ancient mystery societies. Or they may hint at the actual survival of Dionysian rites.

The theater, the temple, the cathedral — each is a mesocosmic symbol, an architectural link between the human being and the universe. For Dionysus, the theater was an ideal temple and performance was a ritual. Some Greek dramas took their pattern from Mystery rites, a practice which extended even to the design of the theater. Early orchestra pits supposedly contained altars to Dionysus. The idea of theater as ritual is one which is tightly interwoven with the myths of Dionysus and the history of his worship. Both comedy and tragedy sprang from Dionysian revels. In theatrical productions, audiences could witness dramatic rituals, often a dramatized form of an important myth.

Drama provided a ready disguise for Dionysian rites as we have seen. But as the persecution of the faith grew, its adherents and their god more often resorted to resistance, subversion, and rebellion. As though it could not be contained by theater walls, an untamed force broke out periodically to challenge assumptions of social and spiritual organization, if not to turn the world upside-down.

## DIONYSUS AS REBEL

Dionysus was depicted by both celebrants and foes as a rebellious figure, upsetting the social order with revelry, madness, orgiastic rites, and psycho-acoustic music. In this role, the god was probably invoked by the rituals of Acéphale in the 20th century — as an agent through which the old world would come unraveled, clearing the way for a drastically changed world. The god and his otherworldy train were frequently construed as a threat to the State. For example, the *Senatus consultatum de Bacchanalibus*, a document condemning the feral religion, was issued by the Roman Senate in 186 BC. It said that Dionysus, known in Rome by his Lydian name, Bacchus, was worshipped with secret rites. Rumors reached the Senate that these activities were not only orgiastic, but that they involved criminal behavior and moral perversion. In response, the Senate outlawed the practice of the religion.

Livy's outraged description of the sect's "defilement" humorously anticipates certain modern controversies. "If you knew the age at which men are initiated, you would be filled not only with pity for them, but with shame. Do you think, citizens, that young men who have taken this oath can be made soldiers? Are they to be trusted with arms when they leave this obscene sanctuary? Are they, defiled by their own and others' sins, to fight in defense of the honor of your wives and children? Every offense prompted by lust, deceit or violence which has been committed in these last years, originated in that shrine. The Evil grows every day. It affects the whole Commonwealth of Rome."[27] Fueled by such inflammatory remarks, the government ultimately persecuted and killed a multitude of those who refused to abandon the religion.

In a letter to Dr. Robert Ornstein, a specialist in the study of altered states of consciousness, Phillip K. Dick made a case for the continuity of the rebellious god's spirit throughout millennia:

> The Qumran men had as their god not the mythical Jesus but the actual Zagreus...a form of Dionysos. Christianity is a later form of the worship of Dionysos, refined through the strange and lovely figure of Orpheus. Orpheus, like Jeses [sic], is real only in the sense that Dionysos is become socialized; born here as a child of another race, not a human but a visiting one race, Zagreus has to learn by degrees to modify his "madness," which is now kept at a low ebb. Basically he is with us to reconstruct us as expressions of him, and the m.o. of this is our being possessed by him — which the early Christians sought for, and hid from the hated Romans. Dionysus-Zagreus-Orpheus-Jesus was always pitted against the City of Iron, be it Rome or Washington D.C.; he is the god of springtime, of new life, of small and helpless creatures, he is the god of mirth and frenzy, and of sitting here day after day working on this novel.[28]

For Dick, the Empire — a malevolent union of church and state — had never ended. People were living in the "Black Iron Prison," as either prisoners or slaves. The Empire had changed its form over the millennia, but it remained much the same as Livy's Rome. Nevertheless, a rescuing/ healing influx of divine living information was at work, according to Dick. He christened it "VALIS," an acronym for Vast Acting Living Intelligence System.

## Three Myths

In early 1974, Dick began to experience unusual episodes which haunted him for the remainder of his too-brief life. To begin with, he claimed that a pink beam of pure information had penetrated his consciousness. It would be easy to dismiss this as a schizoid episode, if the pink beam had not informed Dick that his son required emergency surgery for an invisible, though deadly birth defect. Dick's assessment of the affliction proved to be true and a life-threatening situation was indeed averted. Later, as he grappled with these experiences while working on the novel *VALIS*, Dick wrote:

> Against the Empire is posed the living information...Since the universe is actually composed of information, then it can be said that information will save us. This is the saving *gnosis* which the Gnostics sought. There is no other road to salvation. However, this information — or more precisely the ability to read and understand this information — can only be made available to us by the Holy Spirit. We cannot find it on our own. Thus it is said that we are saved by the grace of God and not by good works, that all salvation belongs to Christ, who, I say, is a physician.[29]

In the novel, *Radio Free Albemuth* (a prototypical version of *VALIS*), he described his vision of Christ in distinctly Dionysian terms:

> Before, the King had come quietly, at the margin of Roman affairs, simply to observe and to teach. He had not wished to be found by the Romans, cornered, tried, and murdered. That was the risk he had run and he had realized it. It was not his intention then to fight; he was King in identity, in spirit, but not in act. He had not died like kings do but as criminals do, in disgrace. In the centuries since his dreadful murder he had lingered on, invisibly, with no body like ours, dancing outside our lives among the rows of newborn corn, dancing in the mists, pale and thin. People had seen him and mistaken him for

> a corn king, for the spirit of new life in the spring, the annual and permanent awakening after the death of winter. He had allowed them to imagine that he was nothing more; these were the centuries when knowledge of his real purpose was virtually lost. Mankind was acclimated to the idea of tyrannical rule. The King was visible only as mist itself, mist dancing in the mist, to bring the new crop to life; as if no men but only the corn now heard his voice.[30]

For Dick, a great awakening was at hand. As people began to act as vehicles for this spirit, everything would change. Humanity would be rescued from history. This experience of transmundane bliss would undermine the authority of bureaucracies and hierarchies by offering mystical empowerment to individuals. Caught up in ecstatic frenzy, each celebrant would become an expression of this divine force on earth. Illusions of worldly authority would lose their meaning in such circumstances, unveiling the Mysteries of Nature which had been suppressed and hidden beneath a thick layer of civilization and its signs. Lacking hierarchy, humanity would become divine and acephalous. Jesus/ Dionysus would permeate the world, uniting heaven and earth.

Such initiates would be reborn into a new realm. The goal of this process appears in the eleven point program of the Acéphale: "Realise the universal fulfillment of the individual being within the ironical world of animals through the revelation of an acéphalous universe, a universe which exists in a state of play rather than one of obligation."[31] If such realizations were to occur on a mass scale, life as we know it would change. This unrestrained epiphany would "lift the curse of those feelings of guilt which oppress men, force them into wars they do not want, and consign them to work from whose fruits they never benefit."[32]

Conversely, those who choose to ignore this Dionysian resurrection or try to smother it with repression must do so at the peril of falling prey to compulsions of madness and violence. "For those who do not close their mind against it, such experience can be a source of spiritual power and eudomonia. But

## Three Myths

those who repress the demand in themselves or refuse its satisfaction to others, transform it by their act into a power of disintegration and destruction."[33] This is the curse of the spell of madness which was cast upon Dionysus by a furious Hera. Out of his mind, he wandered the world with his company of Maenads and Satyrs, engaging in fierce battle wherever he went until he was healed by his grandmother, Rhea, and purified from the violence he had committed through initiation into her Mysteries. Likewise, the mass of humanity awaits a similarly miraculous redemption — the healing of which Dick wrote.

Dionysian rebellion is free to demolish signs, systems, and the very idea that anything can be satisfactorily explained. In order to explore and experiment with the possibilities of life, one must first destroy conditioned thought-forms and their extensions in the phenomenal world. In seeking to understand, we destroy that which we long to know. In *Inner Experience*, written four years after the Acéphale group disbanded, Bataille wrote: "If I said decisively 'I have seen God', that which I see would change. Instead of the inconceivable unknown — wildly free before me, leaving me wild and free before it — there would be a dead object and the thing of the theologian — to which the unknown would be subjugated, for, in the form of God, the obscure unknown which ecstasy reveals is *obliged to subjugate me...*"[34] One does not experience the fire of Dionysus without being consumed by it. This heat melts and reconciles contraries: male and female; god and man; earth and heaven. This is a conflagration that consumes the imprinted forms of consciousness and leaves raw ecstatic bliss in its wake.

"Order, being anti-entropic, requires a fixed and limited context within which to exist," speculative fiction author Norman Spinrad wrote in *Agent of Chaos*. "Chaos contains all such limited contexts within it as insignificant eddies temporarily resisting the basic universal tendency towards increased Social Entropy."[35] In this novel, the Dionysian urge appears in a rebellious context, as the spirit which guides the mysterious Brotherhood of Chaos. Its members aspire to true randomness, a difficult goal since such an undertaking obviously cannot be planned. To live in the instant, splashed in endocrine tides, is to exist as "*illegal* and essentially free beings (the only real *outlaws*),"[36] as Georges Bataille raged in the *Critical Dictionary*. This is the innocent savagery of animals, which can be experienced by humans only through metamorphosis. Inside of every person, Bataille tells us, there is an enslaved animal. When the animal is released, the man dies. Freed from poetic wonder, the animal looks back at the man as a prison and as the embodiment of bureaucracy.

It is known that particular psychedelic sacraments found in the botanical world can induce such spontaneous and even animalistic states of being. These plants and fungi, globally linked with animistic spirituality, have enabled shamans and holy men to transcend imprinted thought-forms for thousands of years. Intoxicated, they visit invisible realms and acquire uncanny wisdom through supernatural initiation. They are capable of seeing through the eyes of animals, as well as those of gods. These sacraments and their mysteries were held sacred by worshippers of Dionysus and Shiva.

## KISS, KISS, BHANG! BHANG!

> "If they approve of your taste in confections, they might also take you along the jelly-bean path and direct you to the famous KEY CLUB OF THE SEVEN ROOMS, kiddingly referred to by the regulars as the 'Gingerbread House.' It contains seven rooms which function around the clock, connected by floor passageways, each room jampacked with indescribable nonsense. There's only one lightbulb for all seven rooms, which is shifted from nook to nook every fifteen minutes by a trained ape of undefined sex. This shouldn't be confused with the LOUNGE OF THE SEVEN PLEASURES..."[37]

Few Arcadian innovators have matched the skill with which the ancient *Mystes*, the hierophants of the Mystery Religions, transported initiates into realms of pure bliss and holy terror. This initiatory transcendence was accomplished with a fascinating assortment of techniques including brainwave-changing sounds,

## Three Myths

manipulation of sexual energies, and sacramental usage of euphoriant plants and psychedelic fungi. The Dionysian ritual acted by overwhelming the initiate's senses from within and without.

Was the sacrament which drove the maenads into their holy frenzy merely wine? In "Food for Centaurs," Robert Graves speculates that psychedelic mushrooms may have fueled Dionysian revels and Mystery rites.

> -Dionysus, who played a part in the Mysteries not only of the Goddesses Demeter and Persephone, but of the Goddess Rhea too, may once have been the Mushroom-god. And the fly amanite may have been the secret agent which sent the maenads raging, with froth on their lips, across the wild hills, tearing in pieces men and beasts — among them Pentheus of Thebes and Orpheus of Macedonia. Pentheus, according to Euripides, had his head wrenched off by Maenads who included his own loving mother Agave. Orpheus suffered the same unusual fate. Since they died as representatives of Dionysus, did it perhaps refer to the necessary removal of the sacred mushroom cap from its stalk? Dionysus' devotees first drank beer, laced with the toxic juice of yellow ivy — hence the sacred ivy wreath — and later took to wine. But they drank this, presumably, to wash down the fiery fragments of mushroom; because to tear even a kid in pieces, such fantastic muscular strength is needed as no beer or wine or mead can provide.[38]

Graves argues that the sacred mushroom may have been banned as a general stimulant by the religious leaders of Greece. He suggests that this sacrament was thereafter reserved for persons of good birth and reputation who qualified for admission into the Mystery Religions.

During the reign of King Erechtheus, who conquered sacred Eleusis and initiated Heracles into its Mystery Religion, the Scirophoria festival of madwomen was held. *Sciros* means both "parasol" and "tumor" in Greek — images that are indeed appropriate for the visionary fungus. In murals painted from this event, one may see the female celebrants and the priest carrying white parasols. Graves states that the parasols depicted are actually vision-inducing mushrooms. Additionally, the mushroom is shaped like the miraculous phallus of the god. These mushrooms were popularly supposed to have sprouted where lightning impregnated the earth. *Amanita muscaria* or psilocybin mushrooms were used to invoke profound states of bliss and terror in Mystery Religion ceremonies. To the celebrant or initiate, the mushroom was the body of the god, to be ritually consumed. This theophagy released the very essence of the god into consciousness. Epiphanies, bliss states, and even revelatory episodes of terror certainly resulted. While in such an altered state, the Mystery initiate *became* the god-man Dionysus. Or, the initiate may have encountered a hierophant who wore and enacted various masks or aspects of Dionysus.

Marijuana continues to enjoy sacramental usage in India, among other places. *Bhang*, a beer brewed from psychoactive hemp, is prominent in the worship of Shiva. It is said to ignite the fire of the soul which burns away illusion and ego. In one story, Shiva comes to rest under a hemp bush following a family argument. Eating the leaves of the plant, he declares it to be his favorite food, thereby becoming the Lord of *Bhang*. This beer is the water of life to devout Shivaites and those who drink it are consuming the god himself.

Those who take this sacrament are cleansed of sin, as are those wandering, *chilum*-smoking *Sadhus* who draw the attention of Shiva and fellow smokers with shouted smoking mantras such as "Bum Shiva!" and "Bam Bam Bholanath!" As the god is perpetually intoxicated by this leafy euphoriant, so are his *sadhus*, who love sharing in his ecstatic state. Achieving this, they become living reverberations of this bliss, accumulators and transmitters of the life-energy. Curiously, smoking cannabis as a sacrament is viewed by *sadhus* as an austerity, since the act is a demonstration of non-attachment to the body. It is also ritually used by practitioners of tantric yoga prior to certain religious sex acts performed in the name of the Goddess Kali.

Notorious 19th century hashish-eater and author Fitz Hugh Ludlow seemed to access this state in his intoxicated reverie. With Dionysian fervor, Ludlow wrote, "-I wandered Bacchus-smitten among the Maenades. Through the viny shades that embowered our dance of rapture, Haliacmon threw the gleam of his sky-bright waters, and the noon rays, sifted through leaves and clusters, fell on us softened like gold into the lap of Danae. Grapes above us, grapes around us, grapes everywhere, made the air as fragrant as a censer. They dropped with the burden of their own sweetness; they shed volatile dews of ecstasy on every sense...Together with troops of Bacchantes I leaped madly among the clusters; I twirled my thyrsus and cried Evoe Bacche with the loudest...I drank the blood of the grapes like nectar; I sang hymns to the son of Semele; I reeled under the possession of the divine afflatus. Around me in endless mazes circled beauteous shapes of men and women; with hands enclasped we danced and sang, and the Maenad houris overshadowed me with their luxuriant disheveled hair."[39]

Presently, the fate of such sacraments looks grim. They have been widely criminalized in the Western world and grouped with recently developed synthetic drugs which can be extremely harmful and addictive. This misunderstanding has contributed to the creation a new scapegoat class — those whose "crimes" are victimless. Despite the fact that such "criminals" do not harm anyone or infringe on the natural rights of others, they are regularly arrested and jailed at an annual cost of $150 billion per year to American taxpayers.

## THE VILLA OF THE MYSTERIES

The essence of the Mystery is found in performing the reenactment of the journey into the underworld, descending into mysterious and frightening depths where mythology and consciousness act upon each other. While much has been lost concerning the nature of these rites, those remnants of information and relics which have survived can be useful in recreating a sense of these initiatory episodes.

## Three Myths

To qualify for such an initiation, the candidate would have been determined to have an intelligible tongue, a kind of righteousness of character and, in some instances, a kind of almost foolish innocence. Once chosen, the candidate would most likely have been instructed by an accomplished Mystes or Hierophant and prepared for immersion in water, the ritual bath of purification. Ceremonial bathing would have taken place at sacred springs which sometimes also served as a temple sites. There the initiate would be baptized in spring water, a symbol of connection with the greater Water of Life.

On the other hand, the idea of bathing in a specially constructed tub can be traced back to ancient Crete, where Dionysus was worshipped as Zagreus. Legend has it that this bath, discovered during the excavation of Crete, was designed for King Minos by Daedalus, the artisan who also designed the King's Labyrinth.

After the ritual of the bath, the neophyte would descend into the lower chambers of a Villa of the Mysteries or a sacred cave, the womb of the Mother Goddess from which the intiate is "born again." In these depths, he or she would find a darkness that enhanced auditory hallucinations just as the architecture of the chambers and sanctuaries was designed to change the nature of sound. And as Dionysus blurs boundaries through paradox and intoxication, so can we imagine the sacrament of the vision-producing mushroom acting on consciousness during this ritual. Sense of time and space would be distorted. In the sensory deprivation of the dark temple, visionary states would be heightened. Perhaps sound would be synaesthetically experienced as light or color. And as one's attention turned inward, the sound of bullroarers would vibrate the body, acting directly on the consciousness of all present, as we will shortly hear. This would signal the choreographed climax to the ritual — the ascension of the initiate to a paradisiacal realm of undifferentiated consciousness; the seed bursting beneath the earth, simultaneously taking root in the darkness and unfurling its leaves to sunlight.

Experimental musician Andrew M. McKenzie describes the function of sacred art in such a ritual:

The strivings to balance life so that an equilibrium is maintained has been attempted through allegorical, representational and exploratory texts, pictures and arrangements of sonic information. The basic premise of this approach is to externalize "problems" (whether solved or not) so that firstly, the problem might be resolved for the creator of the "work" simply by being able to view the situation objectively, and secondly, by presenting it as encoded in a problem to others — their solving it for themselves will enable a direct communication to exist between the creator, the recipient, and in the most noteworthy cases, with all others.[40]

# MUSIC AND MYSTERIUM

The Dionysian bullroarer is an instrument associated with the presence of the god. It generates a thunderous sound as well as an inaudible side-effect: infrasound. Infrasound is a vibration which is felt but not heard. Scientists suggest that this may account for the agitation of animals before thunderstorms and earthquakes. Exposed to infrasound, the initiate experiences something similar, said to be a kind of holy dread. This uncanny sensation is caused by high-intensity sound pressure from the bullroarers. This creates the physical *sense* of having heard something without the perception of any sound. In surviving rituals, this is the voice of the god reaching into the very center of the soul with a resonant vibration. The combination and orchestration of psychoactive elements in such a ritual is quite sophisticated — a spiritual art form known as the Mysterium.

Perhaps more than any other area of creativity, music lends itself to the Dionysiac impulse. Drums, cymbals, bullroarers, the syrinx (also known as the Pan flute), the seven-stringed lyre and the aulos (a kind of double clarinet) were all used to induce a trance of possession by the deity. Such practices continue to persist in the Voduin religion and even resonate in the realm of 20th century pop music. In fact, modern electronic and sampling technology allows musicians to incorporate actual

## Three Myths

sound waves from distant rituals into their works, or even induce trance-states in their listeners

The role of music in the Mysteries can be better understood by considering a scientific phenomenon called entrainment. Entrainment was an effect encountered by businessman and experimentalist Bob Monroe, who studied the impact of sound waves on brain waves. Without realizing it, Monroe stumbled upon one of the primary mechanisms of animistic ritual. Monroe found that brain waves synchronized with rhythms. The listener was able to enter altered states or trance states in this way.

But since the human ear can not detect sounds of less than 40 hertz and most brain wave frequencies fall below that level, Monroe continued to experiment until he developed a system for creating what he called binaural beats. To do this, he used stereophonic headphones to send separate frequencies to each ear. He found that the brain was even able to decode sounds which fell below the threshold of human hearing. One strange side effect of this phenomenon was that it harmonized the brain waves of the right and left hemispheres. Monroe patented this process in 1975, referring to it as frequency following response.

Entrainment of the brain is undoubtedly similar to the state induced by the infrasonic sound pressure generated by the Dionysian bullroarer or the beat of drums. The celebrant exposed to the rhythm or vibration of a god actually experiences the god through the resulting brain-wave state, a state which is shared by everyone within hearing range.

These techniques have been utilized in the field of modern experimental music — an area called psycho-acoustics. Those who listen to this music may choose to do so because it induces trance states, stimulates memory, and even excites the visual cortex. The musical collective T.A.G.C. Research Project is interested in "the occultation of technology." In "T.A.G. Communications an Extension of the Human Nervous System":

> Experiments show that when a person is subjected
> to a short cyclic repetition of external stimulus, the

subject loses contact with the outside world and simultaneously establishes contact with his inner world. The achievement of this inner concentrative state has been practiced by Indian Tantrikas for centuries and recent scientific investigations have revealed this practice to be a direct method of inducing a 'high alpha state.' During the practice of *Kundalini* Yoga, attention is focused in a state of 'One Pointedness' by means of repetitive stimulus, i.e. repetition of such sounds that ultimately incur the creative Alpha state.

In consequence, experts conclude that meditation is neither 'esoteric' or 'Mysterious,' but is a 'practical technique' which uses experiential knowledge based on the actual mechanisms of the nervous system and hence is within the scope of practical applied technology.[41]

For creators of such musical forms, a dynamic involvement is sought with the listener. Such music is an invitation to change and to experience highly personal inner vistas of spirit. Just as Dionysian rhythm and dance were utilized to create ecstatic states of mind and spirit, psycho-acoustic music allows one to directly experience the plurality to be found in varying states of consciousness. Here are the vibrations which evoke the gods of the pagan world. Everything which can be perceived may be rooted in vibration and rhythm. Music suppresses or unleashes forms of consciousness according to its mode. And several of these forms have their own divine personifications. Dionysus, wearing the mask of Shiva, the Lord of Yoga, is the gatekeeper who unites these god-forms.

Earlier in the 20th century, Russian composer Alexander Scriabin had the intuition that exalted states of consciousness could be induced through a combination of music and other sensations. He began working on the idea of creating a ritual of esoteric bliss through sensory overload. Scriabin envisioned an art form that would resonate deeply with its beholders and involve them intimately in a shared ecstasy. It would function like the Mystery Religions on a grand scale, inducing mystical states by over-

## Three Myths

whelming the senses. In his dream of a multi-media passion play, nerve endings would sizzle with transmundane ecstasy as waves of light, music, caresses, heady odors, and exquisite tastes conspired to unhinge workaday consciousness. Scriabin would create his Mysterium — a work of cosmic potency designed to overwhelm its participants. Inducing a crescendo that would catalyze this consensual trance, the Mysterium would become an apocalyptic reconciliation of polarities, resulting in the immersion of all humanity in the glory of a divine consummation and ascension. But in pious humility, Scriabin left the finale of the Mysterium to blossom without him, refusing to compose that part he called "The Seventh Day." This vector, he expected, would play itself out in the hands of some future visionary of expanded capacity. Sadly, the Fates cut Scriabin's work short, blasting him with an abscess of the upper lip which became gangrenous and brought his genius to the very morning of its own Seventh Day.

Being unfinished, the *Mysterium* does not partake of the nature of the closed systems that theology seeks to establish. It becomes a ritual of beauty and bliss, something which is only completed when all participants are overwhelmed and swept up by the sacred. Rooted in music and artful vibration, it slips across barriers of culture and language.

Beyond expressing the emotions of composers and performers to listeners, there are specific instances in which music acts as a psychoactive agent. There are secret societies of initiated *samba* musicians in Brazil. And many Afro-Latin rhythms serve as invitations to gods or goddesses, inducing them to "ride" the bodies of their dancing celebrants. These rhythms — each the signature of a different Voodoo/ Gnostic deity — penetrated the 20th century soundscape and began to spread. Dionysus, a dark stranger with an upright bass, had beaten a new door through the accepted wall of sound with his instrument. Escape was possible. Devotees surrendered to rhythm and were filled with an aspect of spirit. As long as the music played, they shared recontextualized sacred space with each other and with heavenly essences.

## Three Myths

In *Mumbo Jumbo*, Ishmael Reed described the spread of such rhythms in viral terms years before the term "meme" — a unit of cultural imitation or transmission — was coined by Richard Dawkins. Reed noted the viral spread of a music he called Jes Grew, an irresistible outbreak rooted in ragtime music which spread across Prohibition Era America and sparked the Jazz Age. "Dance manias inundate the land. J.A. Rogers writes, 'It is just the epidemic contagiousness of jazz that makes it, like measles, sweep the block.' People do the Charleston the Texas Tommy and other anonymously created symptoms of Jes Grew. The Wallflower Order remembers the 10th century *tarantism* which nearly threatened the survival of the Church. Even Paracelsus, a "radical" who startled the academicians by lecturing in the vernacular, termed these manias 'a disease.'"[42] With the memetic spread of this and other musical strains came encrypted social rituals and secret linguistic forms like Jive. Speaking and singing in an insider language insured that those partaking of the festivities were initiated and trusted insiders. Such secrecy was necessary to protect participants from persecution and prosecution.

> You see the Americans do not know the names of the long and tedious list of deities and rites as we know them. Shorthand is what they know so well. They know this process for they have synthesized the HooDoo of VooDoo. Its blee blop essence; they've isolated the unknown factor which gives the loas their rise. Ragtime. Jazz. Blues. The new thang. That talk you drum from your lips. Your style. What you have here is an experimental art form that all of us believe bears watching. So don't ask me how to catch Jes Grew. Ask Louis Armstrong, Bessie Smith, your poets, your painters, your musicians, ask them how to catch it. Ask those people who be shaking their tambourines impervious to the ridicule they receive from Black and White Atonists, Europe the ghost rattling its chains down the deserted halls of their brains. Ask those little colored urchins who 'make up' those new dance steps and the loa of the Black cook who wrote the last lines of the 'Ballad of

## Three Myths

Jesse James.' Ask the man who, deprived of an electric guitar, picked up a washboard and started to play it. The Rhyming Fool who sits in Re'-mote Mississippi and talks 'crazy' for hours. The dazzling parodying punning mischievous pre-Joycean style-play of your Cakewalking your Calinda your Minstrelsy give-and-take of the ultra-absurd.[43]

In America, Jazz whooped, taunted, and rocked like the Signifying Monkey of African folk-tales. Its sound was a wild and spontaneous one. Like Dionysus, it came from somewhere else and left celebration and dancing in its wake. But other vibrations were rattling the rooftops during this century. Everywhere there were omens of the Parousia, the second coming of Dionysus. New ages and aeons were announced. In Europe, a bizarre art movement bearing the name of a West African vegetation god, Dada, erupted with such intensity that it seemed to signify the end of art and culture. Everywhere people claimed to have seen mysterious lights and airships in the sky. Orson Welles blurred the line between stage magic and theatrical ritual when he convinced thousands of people that the Earth had been invaded by Martians in his notorious "War of the Worlds" radio broadcast. Others told of being abducted by unearthly beings, not unlike the Good People of Irish folklore, and probed, pranked, or instructed. Warfare and its technology became increasingly efficient and impersonal to the point that it was accepted as a new form of entertainment in popular media. Weapons were created to burn, puncture, infect, evaporate, suffocate, and irradiate human beings and anything else in their blast radius. The technology existed to destroy life on a global scale and to transmit sounds and images with digital clarity. LSD was synthesized, catalyzing both the weird mind-control experiments of the CIA and subcultural psychedelic spirituality. Television was invented and soon came to be dominated by progressively fewer vast media cartels. And repeatedly a lusty, crazy joy appeared which could not be contained or suppressed. It traveled like old style religions, from person to person, primarily through the agency of music. The 1960s exploded with Dionysian youth rebellion and wild, electronic, impossible music.

## Three Myths

When the king of Thebes forbade the feeding of Dionysus, the angry loa influenced the young people to revolt. When Proteus, King of Tiryns, closed a temple dedicated to Dionysus known as 'the man of the black goatskin' a contemporary writer described the ensuing choreomania:

*They rushed out of doors and in frenzied dance raged over the countryside, singing weird songs, tearing their garments, unable to stop dancing.*

Dionysus taught the Greeks the Osirian Art which lasted until the Atonists in the late 4th century B.C. convinced the Emperor Constantine to co-sign for the Cross. Dionysus taught the Greek guides to identify the Nature that spoke through mankind. The Work.[44]

To this day, Dionysian revel is prone to spread via such "weird songs" into new cultural contexts. Music is an agent which hops borders without authorization, carrying irresistible messages and enigmas. It is the anti-plague that Ishmael Reed describes. It is the "Fascinatin' Rhythm" which has always traveled faster through dense media, inducing mania as it spreads. It carries the secret word to forbidden places. It changes the mood and the spirit. Everything vibrates and flows through time and consciousness like a song. Listeners enjoy brainwave state rapport. As always, social and spiritual groups still gather to worship the mysteries of rhythm and vibration — connoisseurs of trance states and conviviality.

*Three Myths*

# THE HUMAN JUNGLE

I have untied against you the club-footed vines,
I have sent in the Jungle to swamp out your lines.
The trees — the trees are on you!
The house-beams shall fall,
And the Karela, the bitter Karela,
Shall cover you all!

— from "Mowglis' Song against People" by Rudyard Kipling

Today we are still confronted with the extremes of "the civilized and its light" that so enraged the members of the Acéphale. Many of us live in man-made jungles with new rules and predators. Our conceptions of Nature as city-dwellers are stunted as we spend more and more time in increasingly artificial environments. Nature is fenced off, restricted, and "owned." Artificial light shrouds the stars. Mechanized slaughterhouses take care of the *sparagmos,* the rending to pieces of unseen sacrificial beasts into abstract cuts of meat. Without knowing why or having any choice, we are born into the game of money and the slavery of work. And the once sacred dramatic performance has become fodder for an ever expanding illusory world of electronic media.

Like the infant Dionysus distracted by the Titans with a mirror, millions of human beings are now sitting quietly, enchanted before the magic mirror of television. It no longer matters that the Titans are looming. What matters is the fascinating, though grotesquely distorted, reflection.

Stunned before the television mirror for hours, viewers fall into passive hypnotic brainwave states. Their habit is supported by a global network of satellites, unblinking cathode eyes, and probing video cameras which mimic the human thought process. This system delivers patterns of light and sound to the human brain via the sensorium. Spellbound, the passive "viewers" live vicariously through the images they see. "As part of the masses life is in danger of perishing in random samples, data, markets, or computer nets, or of suffocating in the gigantic tautological machinery of the media industry, that continually sends back the opinions of the masses, that they, as media, formulated."[45]

But could not one reasonably argue that television itself is Dionysian? After all, Dionysus was the god of the theater and drama. And is not the shifting landscape of television a symbolic microcosm of the world? But the passive television state bears little resemblance to the enactment of myth through sacred drama and ritual. As viewers wander through an increasingly dismal, frightening, and illusory landscape, they are bombarded by images and voices urging them to engage in the romance of commerce.

Somewhere in the electronic simulacrum, a *deus ex machina* speaks and the brains of millions of viewers quiver expectantly. Fewer and fewer voices are heard in this illusory world of top-down communication where empires of commerce cavort behind static masks. The Situationist art movement knew this magic mirror and its attendant culture as "The Spectacle," and insisted that it was a device of control. In response, they advocated a revolution of everyday life and insisted that 20th century architects should be building "adventures."

Thanks to the modern mediascape, people experience things which were once the province of schizophrenics — disembodied voices, hallucinatory images, visions of violence. Television violence triggers flight-or-fight instincts with gushes of adrenaline. Such reactions once placed the human being squarely in Nature. But these survival instincts have been rendered useless in the passivity and manipulation of the television trance. Visionary ranter Francis E. Dec, Esq. identified this electronic spectacle as a virtual entity — "the worldwide Computer God" who turns human beings into "parroting puppets" through "Frankenstein Controls." Dec's seeming paranoia is vented in unsettling prose that is reminiscent of the writing of Franz Kafka or Phillip K. Dick. Psychedelic pioneer Dr. Timothy Leary (who was rumored as being acéphalyzed after death in hopes of later achieving a resurrection of his cryogenically frozen head) could almost have been reading from a Dec rant when he stated that those who control the "screens" of the senses control life itself. Or, as Dec would have it: "Primarily, based on your lifelong Frankenstein Radio Controls, especially your Eyesight TV, sight and sound recorded by your brain, your moon brain of the Computer God activates your Frankenstein threshold brainwash radio lifelong, inculcating conformist propaganda, even frightening you and mixing you up and the usual, 'Don't worry about it.'"[46]

There seems to be no doubt that this media world-within-a-world continues to shape the world in which we live. Who controls this recontextualization of experience? Even if we refuse to participate in the illusion, we are subjected to the shared sense of reference that viewers carry with them like a contagious disease.

The memetic infection of television is chillingly explained by Dr. Brian O'Blivion, a character in Director David Cronenberg's film *Videodrome*. "The television screen is the retina of the mind's eye. Therefore, the television screen is part of the physical structure of the brain. Therefore, whatever appears on the television screen emerges as raw experience for those who watch it." Modern theories concerning the manner in which consciousness seems to function appear to reinforce this idea. Our brains limit, edit, and reconstruct what we perceive through our senses, even if this experience is illusory.

Long before television was invented, a fairy tale was written which today sounds like a kind of prophecy. Hans Christian Anderson's "The Snow Queen" revolves around the creation of a magic mirror by a malignant demon. This mirror "had the power of making everything good or beautiful that was reflected in it almost shrink to nothing while everything that was worthless and bad looked increased in size and worse than ever." Attendees of this demon's school boasted that finally everyone could see what the world and man were really like. "They carried the glass about everywhere, till at last there was not a land nor a people who had not been looked at through this distorted mirror." But when they attempted to carry this looking glass to

## Three Myths

Heaven to mock the angels, it grew slippery as they ascended, fell back to earth, and was smashed into millions of fragments. "When one of these tiny atoms flew into a person's eye, it stuck there unknown to him, and from that moment he saw everything through a distorted medium...for even the smallest fragment retained the same power which had belonged to the whole mirror."

Anderson seems to have anticipated electronic media's pall of enchantment, a mesmerizing but distorted reflection of life that pop sociologist Douglas Rushkoff calls "a house of mirrors within mirrors." To Rushkoff, the media mirror is an organism with a kind of life. By observing the operation of this media "organism" — the "datasphere" -one can resist its influence or perhaps even infect it with prankish, heroic, and unauthorized memes — ideological codes which are hidden within "viral shells" of information. These viral shells operate in the same way as the Trojan Horse, concealing an informational surprise within a tasty casing that the media-beast will hungrily devour, allowing the information or disinformation virus to spread. "-DNA is only a code — a language of codons — it directs the physical shape of the future of humanity," Rushkoff tells us. "Likewise those who manipulate the codons of media by launching meme rich viruses are challenging the traditional linear processes by which history is regulated," he argues.[47] But what will such a meme-war in a virtual realm accomplish? There seems to be no act of resistance which cannot be absorbed by the Spectacle and reflected back with a new meaning or as a fashion or product. Instead of reacting with unbridled outrage at such desecration of life, viewers meekly fall into line and imitate what they see in the magic mirror. Dwelling in a meme-polluted artificial wonderland, each viewer yearns to become part of the illusion. And this is literally accomplished as media interpenetrates consciousness and possesses it like a memetic host of demons. To experience one's "15 minutes of fame" is to be validated as real — immortalized in a realm of false light.

As electronic media become increasingly interactive, the escape to man-made realms like the Worldwide Web may prove more seductive than the demands of unmediated life. Cybersex and imaginary computer-pets will even allow users to lavish sexual energy, love and compassion on their computers thus creating new markets for exploitation.

And so we're turned upside-down. We are taught to celebrate busywork — the death of the soul, a game with no end. Like fattened pigeons, we scan the skies for the savior hawk that will deliver us from our favorite shit-stained ledges in a burst of feathers and welcome oblivion. And when the plug is pulled the dream will end. Our cartoonish, force-fed fantasies will dissolve into the graveyard dawn of a ruined world.

# PAROUSIA - THE SECOND COMING OF DIONYSUS

"The power of the Eleusinian Mysteries lay in the fact that they possessed no dogma but, rather, involved certain sacred acts that engendered religious feeling and into which each successive age could project the symbolism that it desired."

— Terrence McKenna, *Food of the Gods*

"It is said that when you move a single pebble on the beach, you can set up a different pattern, and everything in the world is changed. It can also be said that Love can change the future, if it is deep enough, true enough, and selfless enough."

— The Control Voice From *The Outer Limits*

"-it is in the form of cathedrals and palaces that Church and State speak to and impose silence upon the crowds."

— *Encyclopaedia Acéphalica*


Throughout the back pages of history, there have been those who have envisioned Paradise on Earth. Explorers sought it in the blank spaces of maps. Mystics danced to its mysterious rhythms. Social theorists etched heavenly blueprints in the clouds.

## Three Myths

Catching the fever, Henry VI astounded London with an earthly paradise coronation extravaganza which featured the four rivers of Eden, gushing into subterranean chambers, to emerge as rivers of wine while Bacchus, Enoch and Elias observed. As we have seen, establishment of an earthly Utopia was also a central goal of certain Dionysian intiates.

While the sanctuaries of the Mysteries were destroyed long ago, their symbols were perpetuated throughout the ages via art and architecture. "Let us build the most fantastic cathedral imaginable so that those who follow us will look at it and wonder at our madness," an anonymous Spanish architect once proclaimed. The idea of reconfiguring one's environment to create bold new contexts, is nothing less than the endeavor to create psychoactive environmental art which resonates in the hidden landscapes of consciousness and causes changes in life "Everyone will live in their own cathedral," Situationist Ivan Chtcheglov once prophesied. "There will be rooms awakening more vivid fantasies than any drug. There will be houses where it will be impossible not to fall in love. Other houses will prove irresistibly attractive to the benighted traveler."[48] Such environments become a perpetuation of the Mystery, a method of focus which acts on every aspect of the sensorium. And for such architecture and art to exist, its designers must first become living vectors of a bliss which seeks expression through them. "Build therefore your own world," Ralph Waldo Emerson wrote. "As fast as you conform your life to the pure idea in your mind, that will unfold its great proportions."

In Samuel Taylor Coleridge's "Khubla Khan," the poet captured a vision of such great proportions that its very words defied imagination. Like Scriabin's *Mysterium* and the secret society of Acéphale, it remained an unfinished work, since Coleridge's poetic reverie was interrupted by a "person from Porlock." Author Indra Sinha suggests that Coleridge was enjoying and relating a Dionysian theophany, an event which later caused him to be fascinated with the conquest of India by Bacchus. "What is 'Alph' but the holy river Alpheius which ran through the very caverns sacred to Cybele...The poem resounds with the imagery of Siva-Dionysus...Coleridge's description of Kubla Khan's entranced state applies precisely to the intoxicated exaltation of Tantric worshippers."[49] In his own exalted ecstasy, Coleridge conjures a vision which is part blueprint, part invocation, and part evocation. Such work tends to remain unfinished because its completion entails a magnificent rupture from the realm of the imagination into everyday life. Like a magical spell, it seeks expression beyond its source.

> Weave a circle round him thrice
> And close your eyes with holy dread,
> For he on honey-dew hath fed
> And drunk the milk of paradise.

While the actual Kubla Khan may not have worshipped Dionysus, his spirituality included animistic aspects. Under this great Mongolian ruler, the arts and sciences flourished in China and religious tolerance was practiced. This "Wise Khan's" nomadic lifestyle was accommodated by four seasonal palaces. Xanadu was the Summer "palace," which was actually composed of richly decorated yurts. Ruilin — the "Felicitous Forest" of Khubla's pleasure gardens — teemed with game animals, springs, and was crowned with a magnificent pavilion. When he traveled from palace to palace, the Great Khan was borne aloft by four elephants. While the "milk of paradise" in Coleridge's poem sounds exotically intoxicating, it most likely referred to the milk gathered from a stable of 10,000 mares that was poured on the earth by the Khan to appease the spirits when he departed from Xanadu every August 28. The Khan's dynasty was remarkable by the standards of the time because it had a postal service, a large network of roads, and a cosmopolitan population. Xanadu was likened to Heaven by poet Liu Guan. Khubla's love of feasting, pleasure, and intoxication made him the perfect subject for Coleridge's poem. And, it is easy to see how the idea of Khubla's pleasure dome elicits Dionysian thrills in Indra Sinha.

Indeed, any temple of Dionysus must be a pleasure dome, an idea which is barely conceivable to inhabitants of the modern world. It must offer delight and bliss through design, harmonizing and exalting its occupants' relationship to Nature.

## Three Myths

Other locations sacred to the god are marked by the distinct lack of any architecture — the woods and wild places that the deity calls home. There celebrants feel a lusty and intoxicated sense of reverence for the world of Nature. In it they plainly see immanent forms of divine energy. In many ways, Dionysus and Shiva are deifications of the natural world in all of its wild, gorgeous and savage splendor. It is the macrocosm of the world which is the greater temple of the Mysteries, a temple which is alive and aware.

Acéphale utilized two primary sites for their rites, the Place de la Concorde, where Louis XVI was decapitated by guillotine (bureacracy losing its head also Acéphale), and in the depths and the dark woods outside of Saint-Nom. As they sought the forest, celebrants were instructed not to speak to anyone, and to follow directions which would be offered by mysterious strangers. They were allowed to ask no questions as they were directed to a path which left the road, there to walk single file in silence. And they were forbidden to discuss the ritual under any circumstances.

Bataille's description evokes the roots of Acéphale in the ancient Mysteries: "On a marshy soil, in the center of a forest, where turmoil seems to have intervened in the usual order of things, stands a tree struck by lightning. One can recognize in this tree the mute presence of that which has assumed the name of Acéphale, expressed there by these arms without a head. It is a willingness to seek out and to confront a presence that swamps our life of reason which gives to these steps a sense that opposes them to those of others. This ENCOUNTER that is undergone in the forest will be of real value only to the extent to which death makes its presence felt. To go before this presence, is to decide to part the veil with which our own death is shrouded."[50] As with the Mysteries, the effectiveness of the ritual was dependent upon a moment of shock delivered in an appropriate setting, an encounter which would transform the initiate's very image of the world. Afterward, everything would be seen in a new and sacred context and the initiates would become living vectors of the Mystery, something defying description or categorization

## Three Myths

Bataille's intention to penetrate the veil of death was so strong that he actively encouraged one of the members to voluntarily offer himself up as a human sacrifice. Perhaps he desired to celebrate the primal rites of the wild god, the sparagmos of dismemberment which was performed in the mists of antiquity. But if there ever was such a sacrifice, it was not reported or recorded.

In time, the turbulence wrought by World War II caused the sect to disband — another work of sacred art which was cut short and remains only as a mysterious seed. Sometimes, though, such seeds lay dormant underground, waiting for the time to grow, blossom, and bear fruit. And so we may yet see the vastness and beauty of the Pleasure Dome, a renewed expression of sacred architecture. We may be exalted by the seventh day of the *Mysterium*, the climactic Parousia which Scriabin left for other hands to complete. Or we may bear witness to a new Golden Age, spreading like a wildfire of the spirit and waking each and every Finnegan.

Bataille's view of Dionysus and his rites was deeply influenced by the philosophy of Friedrich Nietzsche. And so he would have been familiar with those episodes of Nietzsche's supposed "madness" during which the philosopher claimed to be the incarnation of the god in all his rebellious glory.

Nietzsche wrote to Richard Wagner's wife, Cosima:

> To the Princess Ariadne, my beloved. It is a prejudice that I am a man. But I have often enough lived among men and know all that men can experience from the lowest to the highest. I have been Buddha among the Indians, Dionysus in Greece — Alexander and Caesar are my incarnations, as well as the poet of Shakespeare, Lord Bacon. Lastly I was also Voltaire and Napoleon, perhaps also Richard Wagner....This time, however, I come as the victorious Dionysus, who will make the earth a festival....Not that I have much time....the heavens are joyful that I am there....I have also hung on the cross...[51]

In this letter, Nietzsche touches on the deepest secret of the Dionysian rites — identification with the deity. Such madness is the key to transformation, a closely guarded secret of Western ritual magic. The celebrant must assume the form of the god, himself a hybrid of the human and the divine.

There are many unfinished wings in the Dionysian Pleasure Dome. Here and there, guests may stumble into new spaces where the architecture appears shockingly sacred, yet hideously profane from another perspective. One beholds exhibits, gardens, wonders and dramas which may perform some kind of initiatory function, responding to unconscious desires. In such a place, it is possible to become a child again and see with eyes that have the capacity for wonder. There is a vastness that escapes comprehension, ever expanding and unfolding just beyond the horizon.

But is in the wilds and woods where divine artistry appears undisturbed. In the world of Nature we behold the genius of divinity in an immanent, living Paradise. Without artificial distinctions, we understand that we are also an expression of this savage genius. All of the living world resides within each of us. Like Dionysus and Shiva, we dance the world into existence. We dance madly, intoxicated with love, somewhere beyond the civilized boundaries in the darkest heart of the mighty forest.

# ACKNOWLEDGEMENTS

Many people helped me with this essay and its inspiration, dear friends all. But I would like to offer special thanks to: Christina Gordon; Phillip, Lani, and Zane Walker; Sister Jayne; Forrest Jackson; Sean Richberg; Breck and Sandra Outland; Jason Cohen, proprietor of the amazing Forbidden Books in Dallas; Rodney Perkins; David Hanson; Ean Schuessler; Cody Stromberg; John Freeman, and all of the epopts of the Hot Tub Mystery Religion.

# ENDNOTES

[1] *Programme*, quoted by Alastair Brotchie in Georges Bataille, et al. *Encyclopaedia Acephalica*. London: Atlas Press, 1995.
[2] Ibid.
[3] Ibid.
[4] Fardoulis-Lagrange, Michel. from *Georges Bataille*. by Michael Richardson. London: Routledge Press, 1994.
[5] Ibid.
[6] Nietzsche, Friedrich. *The Portable Nietzsche*.
[7] Ibid.
[8] Blake, William.
[9] Nietzsche. "Jokes, Cunning, and Revenge." *Gay Science* #62.
[10] Allegro, John M. *The Sacred Mushroom and the Cross*. New York: Bantam Books, 1971.
[11] *Shiva Purana, Vidyeshvara Samhita, I, chap. 9, 43-44,* from *Gods of Love and Ecstasy*. By Alain Danielou. Rochester, VT: Inner Traditions, 1982.
[12] Shakespeare, William. *A Midsummer Night's Dream*.
[13] Baigent, Michael and Richard Leigh. *The Temple and the Lodge*. New York: Arcade Publishing, 1989.
[14] Graves, Robert. *The White Goddess*. New York: American Book-Stratford Press, 1948.
[15] Ibid.
[16] Farwell, Byron. *Burton*.
[17] Macoy, Robert, 33 Degree. *General History, Cyclopedia, and Dictionary of Freemasonry*. New York, 1869; cited in Evans-Wentz, W.Y., *The Fairy Faith In Celtic Countries*. Citadel Press: New York, 1994.
[18] Vaneigem, Raoul. *The Movement of the Free Spirit*. New York: Zone Books, 1994.
[19] Novalis
[20] Ibid.
[21] Ibid.
[22] Ibid.
[23] Ibid.
[24] Ibid.
[25] Macbride, J.P., A.S. *Speculative Masonry*. Richmond, VA: Macoy Publishing and Masonic Supply Co., 1971.
[26] Howard, Michael. *The Occult Conspiracy*. Rochester, VT: Destiny Books, 1989.

## Three Myths

[27] Livy from *History of Orgies*.
[28] Dick, Phillip K. *The Selected Letters of Phillip K. Dick, Vol. 4*. Lancaster, PA: Underwood-Miller, 1992.
[29] Dick, Phillip K. *VALIS*, Grafton. Great Britain, 1992.
[30] Dick, Phillip K. *Radio Free Albemuth*. New York: Avon Books, 1985.
[31] *Acéphale*
[32] Ibid.
[33] Dodds, Prof. E.R., quoted from, *Sacred Sexuality*. by A.T. Mann and Jane Lyle. Rockport, MA: Element Books, 1995.
[34] Bataille, Georges. *Inner Experience*. State University of New York Press, 1988.
[35] Spinrad, Norman. *Agent of Chaos*. New York: Belmont Books, 1967.
[36] Bataille. *Critical Dictionary*.
[37] Petronius. *New York Unexpurgated*.
[38] Graves, Robert. *Food For Centaurs*. Garden City: Doubleday, 1960.
[39] Ludlow, Fitz Hugh. *The Hasheesh Eater*. San Francisco: City Lights Books, 1979.
[40] The Hafler Trio, *Plucking feathers from a bald frog*. Stockholm: Psychick Release Production Cerebrum & Press, 1991.
[41] "T.A.G. Communications — An Extension of the Central Nervous System," Glasgow, Scotland: Copyright Anterior, appearing in *Total*, Vol. 1, Spring 1991.
[42] Reed, Ishmael. *Mumbo Jumbo*. New York: Atheneum, 1972.
[43] Ibid.
[44] Ibid.
[45] Szepanski, Adam. "In The Beginning Is The Storm," (liner notes to *In Memorium Gilles Deleuze*, 2 CD set, Mille Plateaux, 1996).
[46] Kossy, Donna. *Kooks*. Portland, OR: Feral House, 1994.
[47] Rushkoff, Douglas. *Media Virus*. New York: Ballantine Books, 1994.
[48] Chtcheglov, Ivan. "Formula For A New City," quoted in *What Is Situationism? A Reader*. San Francisco: AK Press, 1996.
[49] Sinha, Indra. *The Great Book of Tantra*. Rochester VT: Destiny Books, 1993.
[50] Bataille. *Encyclopaedia Acephalica*.
[51] Crawford, Claudia. *To Nietzsche: Dionysus I love you! Ariadne*. State University of New York Press, 1995.

# BIBLIOGRAPHY

Alexander, Caroline. *The Way to Xanadu*. New York: Knopf, 1993.

Anderson, Hans Christian. *The Complete Hans Christian Anderson*, Avenel: Gramercy Books, 1984.

Baigent, Michael, Richard Leigh, Henry Lincoln. *Holy Blood, Holy Grail*. New York: Dell, 1983.

Baigent, Michael. *The Temple and the Lodge*. New York: Arcade, 1989.

Bainbridge, William Sims. *Satan's Power*. Berkeley: University of California Press, 1978.

Barber, Malcolm. *The Trial of the Templars*. Cambridge: Cambridge University Press, 1978.

Baring, Anne. *The Myth of the Goddess*. London: Penguin Books, 1993.

Barton, Blanche. *The Secret Life of a Satanist*. Los Angeles: Feral House, 1990.

Bennett, Chris. *Green Gold The Tree of Life: Marijuana in Magic and Religion*. Frazier Park: Access Unlimited, 1995.

Blake, William. *The Complete Poetry & Prose of William Blake*. Doubleday, 1988.

Brodie, Richard. *Virus of the Mind*. Seattle: Integral Press, 1996.

Budge, Sir Wallis. (translator) The Egyptian Book of the Dead. New York: Carol Publishing Group, 1994.

Burman, Edward. *The Templars. Knights of God*. Rochester, VT: Destiny Books, 1986. p. 80.

## Three Myths

*Cambridge Atlas of Astronomy, The.* Press Syndicate of the University of Cambridge, 1996.

Carpenter, Christopher H. (Ed.) *Masks of Dionysus*, Ithaca: Cornell University Press.

Barber, Richard (Ed.) *Man, Myth and Magic.* BPC Publishing Ltd., 1970.

Charbonneau-Lassay, Louis. *The Bestiary of Christ.* Penguin Books, 1992.

Cocteau, Jean. "Garuda: From Myth to National Symbol." from *ArchipelaGO* magazine. Vol.1 No.1, 1995.

Cooper, J.C. *An Illustrated Encyclopaedia of Traditional Symbols.* New York: Thames and Hudson, 1978.

Crawford, Claudia. *To Nietzsche: Dionysus I Love You! Ariadne.* Albany: State University of New York Press, 1995.

Crowley, Aiwass, and Ra-Hoor-Khuit. *The Book of the Law.* Manuscript 1904.

Crowley, Aleister. "Liber A'ash, vel Capricorni Pneumatici." In *Portable Darkness* edited by Scott Michaelsen. New York: Harmony Books, 1989.

Danielou, Alain. *Gods of Love and Ecstasy.* Rochester: Inner Traditions, 1992.

Daraul, Arkon [pseudonym of Idries Shah]. *A History of Secret Societies.* Secaucus, NJ: Citadel Press, 1961.

Delumeau, Jean. *Sin and Fear.* New York: St. Martin's Press, 1990.

Dick, Phillip K. Radio Free Albemuth. New York: Arbor House, 1985.

Dick, Phillip K. VALIS. New York: Bantam Books, 1981.

Dyczkowski, Mark S.G. *The Doctrine of Vibration*. Albany: State University of New York Press, 1987.

Eliade, Mircea. *A History of Religious Ideas, Vol. 2: From Gautama Buddha to the Triumph of Christianity*. Chicago: The University of Chicago Press, 1982.

*Encyclopaedia Britannica*. (15th Ed.) Encyclopaedia Britannica Inc., 1983.

Evans-Wentz, W.Y. *The Fairy Faith in Celtic Countries*. New York: Citadel Press, 1994.

Feuerstein, Georg. *Sacred Sexuality: Living the Vision of the Erotic Spirit*. New York: St. Martin's Press, 1992.

Frankel, Ellen. *The Classic Tales: 4,000 Years of Jewish Lore*. Northvale, NJ: Jason Aronson Inc., 1989.

Graves, Robert. *Food for Centaurs*. Garden City: Doubleday, 1960.

Graves, Robert. *The White Goddess: A historical grammar of poetic myth*. New York: Creative Age Press, 1948.

Gilmore, Peter H. "Satanism: the Feared Religion" from *http://webpages.marshall.edu/~allen12/feared.txt*, quoted on July 11, 1997.

Grant, Kennth. *Aleister Crowley and the Hidden God*. New York: Samuel Weiser, 1974.

Grant, Kenneth. *Cults of the Shadow*. Samuel Weiser, 1976

Howard, Michael. *The Occult Conspiracy*. Rochester, VT: Destiny Books, 1989.

Hutchison, Michael. *Mega Brain: New Tools and Techniques For Brain Growth and Mind Expansion*. New York: Ballantine, 1991.

Introvigne, Massimo. "Ordeal by Fire: The Tragedy of the Solar Temple." in *Religion* Vol. 25 #3. London: Academic Press, 1995.

Jones, Prudence and Nigel Pennick. *A History of Pagan Europe*. London: Routledge, 1995.

Korbe, Kenneth. *Photo Journalism: The Professional Approach*. (3rd Ed.) Focal Press, 1996.

Kossy, Donna. *Kooks: A Guide to the Outer Limits of Human Belief*. Portland: Feral House, 1994.

Kraig, Donald Michael. Modern Magick. St. Paul, MN: Llewellyn Publications, 1988.

Kripal, Jeffery J. *Kali's Child: The Mystical and the Erotic in the Life and Teachings of Ramakrishna*. Chicago: University of Chicago Press, 1995.

LaVey, Anton Szandor. *The Satanic Bible*. New York: Avon Books, 1969.

LaVey, Anton Szandor. *The Satanic Rituals*. New York: Avon Books, 1972.

Leary, Timothy, Ralph Metzner, and Gunther M. Weil. *The Psychedelic Reader*. New Hyde Park: University Books, 1965.

Lerner, Robert. *The Heresy of the Free Spirit in the Middle Ages*. University of Notre Dame Press, 1972.

Levi, Eliphas. *Transcendental Magic: Its Doctrine and Ritual*. Translated by A. E. Waite. London: Braken Books, 1995.

Ludlow, Fitzhugh. *The Hashish Eater*. San Francisco: City Lights, 1979.

Mander, Jerry. *In The Absence of the Sacred*. San Francisco: Sierra Club Books, 1991.

Marcus, Greil. *Lipstick Traces: A Secret History of the Twentieth Century.* Cambridge: Harvard University Press, 1989.

Michelet, M. *Proces de Templiers.* Paris, 1851.

Milton, John. *The Complete Poetry of John Milton.* Doubleday, 1971.

O'Flaherty, Wendy Doniger. *Siva: The Erotic Ascetic.* London: Oxford University Press, 1973.

Page, Michael and Robert Ingpen. *The Time-Life Encyclopedia of Things That Never Were.* New York: Viking Penguin Inc., 1985.

Partner, Peter. *The Murdered Magicians.* New York: Barnes & Noble Books, 1987.

Partridge, Burgo, *A History of Orgies.* New York: Bonanza, 1960.

Pike, Albert. *Morals and Dogma: of the Ancient and Accepted Scottish Rite of Freemasonry.* Richmond: L.H. Jenkins, 1950.

*Process on Death.* Number 6, 1971.

*Process on Fear.* Number 5, 1970.

Reed, Ishmael *Mumbo Jumbo.* New York: Atheneum, 1972.

Roob, Alexander. *Alchemy & Mysticism.* Benedikt Taschen Verlag, 1997.

Rouget, Gilbert. *Music and Trance: A Theory of the Relations between Music and Possession.* Chicago: The University of Chicago Press, 1985.

Schonfield, Hugh. *The Essene Odyssey.* Element Books, 1984.

Shah, Idries. *The Sufis.* Garden City: Anchor Books, 1971.

Spinrad, Norman. *Agent of Chaos.* New York: Belmont, 1967.

## Three Myths

Stafford, Peter. *Psychedelics Encyclopedia*. Berkeley: Ronin Publishing, 1992.

Swezey, Stuart. *Amok Journal*, Los Angeles: Amok, 1995.

Tame, David. *The Secret Power of Music*. New York: Destiny Books, 1984.

Vaneigem, Raoul. *The Movement of the Free Spirit*. New York: Zone Books, 1994.

Wang, Robert. *The Qabalistic Tarot*. York Beach: Samuel Weiser, 1983.

Wood, David. *Genisis*. Tunbridge Wells, Kent: Baton Press, 1985.

Wilson, Colin. *The God of the Labyrinth*. Panther Books, 1977.

Wright. *Narratives of Sorcery and Magic*. Quoted from *An Encyclopedia of Occultism* by Lewis Spence. New York: Citadel Press, 1993.